OUR THREATENED VALUES

RECEIVING GERMAN PRISONERS IN THE FIELD
PANEL FROM TRIUMPHAL ARCH.

NOTE ON ILLUSTRATION

This is one of twelve panels from the Triumphal Arch of Marcus, erected on the Capitol in 176 in honour of the double conquest of Germans and Sarmatians. It represents two German captives brought in by a praetorian guard. They are begging the Emperor's mercy, which the protective gesture of his hand shews is being granted. The face of Marcus is grave and sad.

The illustration and the above note are reproduced, by kind permission of the publishers, from the Loeb edition of Marcus Aurelius.

FOR MY DEAR LIVIA

"*And thou shalt teach them diligently unto thy children*"

OUR THREATENED VALUES

by

VICTOR GOLLANCZ

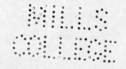
LONDON
VICTOR GOLLANCZ LTD
14 HENRIETTA STREET, W.C.2

FIRST PUBLISHED, JUNE 1946
SECOND IMPRESSION, JUNE 1946
THIRD IMPRESSION, JULY 1946
FOURTH IMPRESSION, JULY 1946

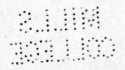
Made and Printed in England by The Cornwall Press Ltd., Paris Garden, London, S.E.1.

OUR THREATENED VALUES

An hour before I sat down to write this essay I read extracts from a speech made the previous evening by Field-marshal Viscount Montgomery. "The German food-cuts have come to stay," he is reported to have said. "We will keep them at 1,000 calories (Britons get 2,800). They gave the inmates of Belsen only 800." These words reveal—they could not have revealed more clearly if they had been spoken for the purpose—the moral crisis with which western civilisation is faced.

I doubt whether even a thoughtful minority realises how grave that crisis is. Most of us are uneasy, and a few of us are downright frightened, about the atom bomb: we feel that another war, far more painful and degrading than the last, may sooner or later be upon us. For my part, I think the danger is exaggerated. Of course, it is there; and whether in the day by day exchanges of diplomacy or in the longer-term devising of international constitutions, no effort for nullifying it can be too great or too single-minded. For all that, I think it possible, and even probable, that there will never be another "great" war. The more pressing danger is of a different kind: it is nothing less than that the typical values of western civilisation may so nearly vanish—they can never, from their nature, vanish entirely—as no longer to contribute to what Mr. Churchill has called "the forward march" of mankind. And if war does come, it will not come, essentially, because the machinery for preventing it is imperfect: it will come because day by day those impulses in our hearts which make for strife are being strengthened, and those which make for harmony are growing weaker. At the crucial moment it will not be paper constitutions that men and women will obey: they will obey their own nature, and their own nature such as it has become.

I shall try in this essay to set out what I have called the typical values of western civilisation, to give some examples of the ways in which they are being progressively threatened, and to suggest how the danger can best be met. There will be nothing new

7

in what I have to say, nor can I hope to say it in a new manner; my less ambitious purpose will be merely to remind: to bring back to the thought of men and women things they have known but have forgotten, and to suggest to others who indeed still remember them but remember them, in the stress of daily affairs, without Blake's sense of mental fight, that these are matters, spiritually as well as physically, of life or death.

But first let me excuse myself for what may appear to be an offensive discrimination implied by the phrase "the typical values of western civilisation." I may speak of the West—by which I mean Europe, and this island, and the civilisations which have developed from them—because for fifty three years I have lived and had my being in it: I know it as I knew my mother and as I know my wife. Of other civilisations I know only from books, and little enough from them. It is certain that a devotion to these values in a rather different form, and perhaps a purer devotion than in Europe, is to be found in other civilisations also. But I can speak only of what I intimately know: and, what is more to the point, western civilisation will influence the world, for good or evil, as long as the mind can foresee, notwithstanding the growing influence of the Soviet Union and the potential influence, no less immense, of the emergent East. If the influence of the West is to be for good, it is essential that she should preserve her values, not for herself alone but for the world.

Another misunderstanding is possible. I said that I should try to set out the typical values of western civilisation, and to give some examples of the ways in which they were being progressively threatened. The implication might seem to be that for centuries these values have been the rule in western civilisation. That, alas, is very far from my meaning. No one who has turned over the pages of European history, and been appalled by its record of tyranny and ruthlessness and greed, could conceivably come to so pleasant a conclusion. I mean something quite different. I mean that patchily, haltingly, with advances here and set-backs there—sometimes with whole areas sunk for generations in all but complete barbarism, and sometimes with a quick blossoming, perhaps in one small island, of the human spirit—these values had steadily, with whatever painful slowness, been winning acceptance. The general direction had been unmistakable. Moreover, in the area of western civilisation as a whole the deliberate and self-conscious denial of these values had long been becoming, until a comparatively recent date, increasingly rare. Sometimes, indeed, it was the very devotion to these values, the final implications of which were little understood, that hindered the advance : more commonly, it was simply that the lump was big and the leaven small.

And now, I believe, the whole process is in danger of being reversed. Fewer and fewer men fight for these values : more and more let them go by default : and more and more either imply or openly proclaim a belief in their contraries.

I

Our central value—or, to put it in another way, the value that includes all our other values—is respect for personality.

It is important to understand precisely what is meant, in this phrase, by the word "respect" and the word "personality." Respect does not mean (as it means when used with a narrower significance) admiring, or fearing, or looking up to, or dutifully obeying, or regarding as good, or recognising as superior in character or intellect or station ; nor does it mean some or all of these attitudes, or of similar attitudes, combined in various proportions. And "personality" does not mean "certain selected personalities."

Negatively, respect for personality can be understood by reflecting on a statement which uses the word "respect" in one of the narrower senses. Consider, for instance, the phrase "I respect my father." If anyone who said that were asked "Why? " he would probably answer "Because he's my father." Further pressed, he might insist that the reason was sufficient, or might be prepared to amend his reply to "Because he's a good father." Similarly, a man might say "I respect the King: because he's the King: because he has carried out with courage and devotion the duties of a constitutional monarch." Or, rather differently, "I respect Mr. Churchill, not because he was Prime Minister nor yet because I agree with his politics, but because during the most critical years of our history, and with a burden of responsibility such as no other Englishman has ever borne, he had the faith of a child and the heart of a lion."

Now the very fact that in these sentences my father, the King, and Mr. Churchill are *selected* as objects of respect shows

9

that the word "respect" is being used in a sense other and narrower than that which we intend when we speak of "respect for personality": and this at once becomes apparent when such reasons as "because he's my father" or "because he's a good father" are adduced in explanation. The very reason for which we respect them in the broader sense would itself preclude us from *particularizing* them for respect in that sense. I personally do in fact respect, in the narrower sense also, all three of them; but if I were asked "Why do you respect your father, and the King, and Mr. Churchill?", and if I understood that respect in the broader sense were intended, my reply in all three cases would be the same, namely "because he's a personality."

When we say that we respect personality, we mean that we recognize in every human being, and to a certain extent (or even completely, perhaps) in every living thing, something special, particular, concrete, individual, unique: something, as the Greeks would have said, αὐτὸ καθ' αὑτὸ : something—and this is perhaps the nearest that can be got to expressing what from its very nature must elude definition—something in its own right. There is in every human being, we say, something as much in *its* own right as my self-consciousness tells me I am in *mine*.

As much as I am in mine, but no more; for I also am a personality that I must respect. Fénelon, anticipating Freud (as so often theology, from its different approach, anticipated modern psychology) said somewhere that we should be in charity with ourselves as well as with our neighbours. There is indeed nothing self-abasing in respect for personality. In spite of *accidental* differences, and very wide ones, in spiritual development—the difference, for instance, between St. Francis at one end of the scale and Herr Streicher at the other; in spite, too, of greatly varying levels of capacity and intellect: respect for personality recognises the *essential* spiritual equality of all human beings, including ourselves, and perhaps of every living thing.

If I have made myself clear, it must at once be apparent that the real test of respect for personality is our attitude towards people we "don't like", towards those whom, in the narrower sense, we "don't respect", and to all whom we think of as enemies or criminals or sinners. To be concrete, the test was our attitude, during the war, to Germans and Italians and Japanese; was our attitude, a few months ago, to John Amery and William Joyce; is our attitude, as I write this, to

Goering and Ribbentrop and Streicher and the rest. To talk of Huns and Wops: to rejoice when Joyce and Amery are sentenced to a shameful end: to think with pleasurable triumph of those wretched men in the dock at Nuremberg—all this is to blaspheme against respect for personality.

I remember reading as a boy something written by Oscar Wilde—I think it is in *De Profundis*—which made a profound impression on me. Wilde had been tried and sentenced; and as he left the dock for prison, when everywhere around him was an atmosphere of hostility and contempt, a bearded stranger, whom he was never to see again, raised his hat in salutation. He did this, I like to think, not because he sympathised with Wilde's practices, nor because he disapproved of the sentence, but as a simple act of respect to a fellow human being in torment. And when I read what the Press had to say about Joyce and Amery the memory of that passage came back to me, and I hoped that there were perhaps one or two who on those occasions did likewise.

Only one person on earth, so far as the records go, has shown a respect for personality utter and without reservation. Christ consorted with harlots and sinners neither in condescension nor without recognition of their sins: he thought of them quite naturally, quite as a matter of course one might say, as fellow human beings, and therefore, to him as a man, essentially and beyond their sins his equals. "Why callest thou me good?" he asked: "there is none good but one, that is, God." And he preached respect for personality in words of a beauty and conviction which never have been and never can be surpassed. There is some great music—Beethoven's Fifth Symphony, for instance—which over-familiarity has spoiled: only when a Toscanini conducts it, or when there is a magic fitting of the music to our need, does it mean for us what it meant when we were young and freshly receptive to its message. So only when they are spoken by a voice of great spiritual power, or when at some climax of disgrace, such as Belsen or Hiroshima, we fly to what may save us from terror and despair—only at moments such as these do we experience once again the full revelation of verses which teach respect for personality in its ultimate form—the verses which begin with the words "But I say unto you, love your enemies".

But *why*, it may be asked, should we respect personality—not this or that personality, but personality as such? What is the sanction? There are many answers: one, and an obvious one, would be given by pantheism, and others by various systems of eastern wisdom and western philosophy. But there are two answers, I think, which come naturally to people trained in the European tradition; and they are not, as will be seen, mutually exclusive. They may be loosely called the religious and the non-religious.

In western religious thought, respect for personality is demanded by three interrelated religious doctrines: that God created all men in His own image, that God is the Father of all men, and that all men are therefore brothers. Both before and after the birth of Christianity, Judaism—prophetic, talmudic and cabbalistic—insisted on this Fatherhood of God and brotherhood of men. "Are ye not" cries the prophet Amos—"Are ye not as children of the Ethiopians unto me, O children of Israel? saith the Lord. Have not I brought up Israel out of the land of Egypt? and the Philistines from Caphtor, and the Syrians from Kir?" Which is as if a modern Jew or Russian, or some refugee from Lidice, were to ask, in spite of all the wrong that had been done to him, "Is not my God also the God of the Nazis?" There is a legend in the Talmud which is remarkable not so much for what it says as for the light it throws on the religious consciousness of men who, regarding Egypt as the national enemy, could nevertheless invent it. The story runs like this: that when the Egyptians were drowning in the Red Sea, and Miriam was singing her song of triumph and thanksgiving, the angels in heaven began to take up the refrain; but God stopped them, saying "What? My children are drowning, and ye would rejoice?" To this day orthodox Jews preserve the memory of that legend. It is customary on all joyful occasions to sing the Hallel, or song of praise. But during Passover, which commemorates the deliverance from Egypt, it is sung in full only on the first three days; on the four remaining days it is sung in a shortened form, because some thirty three centuries ago the Egyptians, who were also God's children, were destroyed. In the same spirit, but even more directly, the Cabbala insists that every man, however sinful, is in some degree divine. With that mixture of nonsense and profound wisdom which is characteristic of it, it relates that God has divided Himself and placed a particle of Himself in the soul of every human being: and that there it will remain, pure and undefiled no matter how wicked the individual may be, until men, reuniting with one another in perfect brotherhood, recreate at last the Unity of God.

But it was Christ who was to experience the universality of God's Fatherhood with a directness and immediacy never approached before or since. Or if that is too bold a claim, for no one can know what is in other men's hearts, it is at least true to say that he alone has had the power to communicate some measure of this experience to countless others. "Are not two sparrows" he asked, "sold for a farthing? and one of them shall not fall on the ground without your Father." I have already suggested that in the injunction to love our enemies respect for personality finds its ultimate expression. And we are immediately told *why* we should love our enemies: "That ye may be the children of your Father which is in heaven: for he maketh his sun to rise on the evil and on the good, and sendeth rain on the just and on the unjust." These few words, so rebuking to the self-righteous, are the greatest of all Christ's gifts—the greatest of all the gifts, I would dare to say, of Hebrew prophecy—to the religion of the western world.

The non-religious man of our tradition, if asked why we should respect personality, would give a different answer, though many may think that it is in the last analysis the same. I recognize (he would say), with a sense of necessity or inevitability independent of logical processes, my own uniqueness, my own "being in my own right." I recognize that there is in me an inner citadel that must be for ever inviolate. And because I recognize this I understand, by imaginative sympathy, that what is true of me is true of others: that every human being is unique, and has a citadel which is sacred: and that I must imperatively respect in others what I know, from the very nature of my being, must be respected in me.

* * * *

Before I pass on, a possible misconception should be removed. Does not an insistence that every personality is "in its own right" imply, it may be asked, that egoism and the pursuit of self-interest are admissible or even desirable?

The very contrary is the case. In every human being there are two competing impulses: the impulse to assert oneself, and the impulse to cooperate with others. Greed, selfishness, cruelty, and the pursuit of power are modes of the first: any practice of charity, mercy or service is a mode of the second. All hatred, even if unaccompanied by what is ordinarily called an act, is spiritual self-assertion, just as all love, even when similarly unaccompanied, is spiritual cooperation. It is unnecessary for the present purpose to attempt any analysis of these two impulses: to consider, for instance, what are their origins, and whether they are in fact modes of, or developments from, something more fundamental than either. For my own part, I believe with some Freudian revisionists, and even, if I remember rightly, with the later Freud himself, that both these impulses are, so far as human nature is concerned, independent: and Jewish theology, with its duality of the good and evil instinct, as well as much but not all Christian theology, would agree. However that may be, we have only to look into our own hearts to know that we are indeed a battle-ground for these two competing impulses, and we have only to observe our neighbours to realise that in this respect we are by no means singular.

It cannot be doubted that the art of civilisation consists, on the one hand, in partly curbing and partly sublimating the impulse of self-assertion, and on the other in strengthening the impulse of cooperation and in extending the area of its activity. Such an endeavour is imperatively demanded by respect for personality. Self-assertion necessarily involves physical or spiritual aggression against others : it tampers with, it stunts or warps, their personality; whereas cooperation not only leaves others free to express and develop their personality, but it positively helps them to do so. Where self-assertion rules, all is negative : either everyone striving with and thwarting everyone else, or perhaps, in the upshot, the many enslaved, spiritually and physically, to the few. Where cooperation rules, all is positive : every seed coming to its own perfect flower in the garden of life.

And the curbing of self-assertion and development of cooperation is demanded by respect for the personality not only of others but also of ourselves. For self-assertion—all egoism, greed, hatred, lust and aggression—is sterile and corrupting: "an expense of spirit in a waste of shame." The end is ashes in the mouth and ice in the heart. Whereas by a beautiful alchemy, which may suggest to us very dimly the hidden meaning of Unity and the Whole, the practice of selfless cooperation ministers, as nothing else can minister, to the serene development of our own personality. That is, of course, what is meant by the saying "Whosoever shall seek to save his life shall lose it; and whosoever shall lose his life shall preserve it."

The ideal society, it may be said, is one of fully developed personalities, freely cooperating, but each one of them with an inner core of unassailable loneliness.

II

Respect for personality, our value of values, is today everywhere threatened. In thought, in speech, in act it suffers hourly dishonour. I must repeat that this, and not the atom bomb, is the major threat to our civilisation.

It is in fascism, of course, that contempt for personality reaches its final expression; for it passes beyond contempt, and becomes hatred. Under the Nazis the values of western civilisation were not merely disregarded, they were reversed: good became evil, and evil good. That a man had rights simply because he was a man: that the free development of individuals was something intrinsically to be desired: that equality and variety were the goals of social endeavour—all such ideas were not merely contemptuously dismissed as liberal, Jewish or Marxist, but were spat upon as wicked. For the real horror of Nazism was not that it was evil—there had been hideously evil régimes time and again in the world's history: the real, the new horror was that it made a religion of evil. "If therefore the light that is in thee be darkness, how great is that darkness!"

And yet I must say this, even at the risk of seeming to talk nonsense and very pernicious nonsense at that: monsters though the Nazis were, and unspeakably evil though the things they thought and did, there was some spark of goodness even in the worst of them. In Streicher himself there was—how dare I put it?—potentiality of a sort: it was the same thrusting something which makes men saints that made of him, with his history and environment and mental and physical constitution, not even a great sinner but just a sordid little gangster sadist. This is why, though he is in one sense lower than the beasts, he is in another sense higher: and this is why, also, while we can pity a beast only for its sensations we can pity him for something more.

However that may be, you will find the religion of evil in every phase of Nazi life and policy. The two foundations of the system were *Gleichschaltung*—conformity, an absolute dictation, not only of what men should do, but of what they should think—and Power—the hierarchical exercise of absolute power by some men over others. Justice was what the Führer thought; and the police, who should be the servants of established law, became the Gestapo, an instrument of arbitrary terror. Accompanying it all was a cult of ruthlessness and cruelty and war, not—which would have been vile enough—as necessary instruments of policy, but as things supremely good and wholesome in themselves.

And in the end millions upon millions of men and women and children with minds to fear and nerves to suffer; millions upon millions of breathing creatures with a right to life and happiness; millions upon millions of individuals with who can say what precious potentialities yet unfulfilled—they were sent, now mere ciphers, to the gas and flames, and in a moment the heirs of creation were nothing.

Hitler is dead, and Germany is in ruins. But has the horror passed? I do not think so. Nazism was not an isolated phenomenon; it was merely the final expression, so far, of tendencies which had for a long time been growing stronger. Those tendencies are still at work; some of them are more widespread than ever; and even here in England there are disquieting signs that respect for personality, which we have guarded, and in spite of everything still guard, more devotedly perhaps than any other people, is growing weaker.

III

While I by no means under-estimate the dangers of a resurgent fascism in many parts of the world, and particularly, owing to our own follies, in Germany, I am certain that it is in the spread of what is today called communism, and in the growing power throughout Europe of Soviet Russia, that the strongest positive forces opposed to the stability and development of our western civilisation are now to be found. I am certain also that British behaviour towards Germany, or British acquiescence, willing or unwilling, in the behaviour towards her of others, is doing more than anything else to facilitate the spread of communism and to strengthen the power of the Soviet Union. It is therefore to these two topics that the major part of this short essay will be devoted.

As I write these words I hear a droning both on the right of me and on what may be courteously called the extreme left. The words are the same but the accents are different. "Anti-soviet" murmurs the right, with a slightly suspicious approval. "Anti-soviet" mutters the left, in tones varying from pained surprise to fanatical hatred. Cannot this sort of stupidity be done with once and for all? I am neither pro-soviet nor anti-soviet, neither pro-German nor anti-German, neither pro-French nor anti-French: I am, I hope, pro-humanity. What anyhow is "anti-soviet" supposed to imply? Dislike of the Russian people? But I have found them charming. Dislike of what their statesmen are doing? Yes, but it is question only of degree: I dislike what nearly all statesmen are doing. Dislike of their final aims? On the contrary, I passionately approve of them, if indeed they any longer *are* their aims. Dislike of their methods? Not merely dislike, but detestation: that is what this essay is largely about. Intolerance of them, then, because they use these methods? Not in the least: though I am no doubt as weak in my efforts to be tolerant as the next man, I regard all intolerance as abominable. So much, but no more, ought to be said immediately: I shall hope to make my position clearer later on.

An even graver misunderstanding must be removed without a moment's delay; for unless I am careful the right will be welcoming me, and the left spurning me, as a renegade from socialism. They could not make a stupider mistake. I have said that the curbing of self-interest and the development of co-operation is demanded by respect for the personality not only of others but also of ourselves. That is only another way of saying that respect for personality, to be complete, demands the super-session of capitalism by socialism. It demands more than that: it demands, in the end, the establishment of a genuinely communist society, in which each will give according to his ability and each will receive according to his need. The real case for socialism is not economic at all, but moral. For capitalism—the pursuit of private profit—consecrates self-interest and greed over a large area of daily life: it recognises them as the normal and respectable motives that not merely actuate but ought to actuate a man in the regular business of earning his bread. It therefore strengthens the self-regarding elements in his nature, instead of weakening or sublimating them. How can anyone, whether capitalist or worker, be wholeheartedly an altruist if he is constantly thinking in the workshop or office of how he can get the most for himself from the available resources? The thing simply cannot be done : it in fact isn't done : and this business self-interest tends to set the whole tone of national life, and to communicate itself to those who are not directly or indirectly concerned with business in any form. Even the arguments in favour of socialism that appear to be economic are really moral : if we argue that socialism will bring material prosperity, we do so, or ought to do so, not because material prosperity is intrinsically desirable, but because poverty and insecurity degrade personality. Subject, indeed, to the reservation just implied, a poorer society of men and women freely cooperating in mutual aid would be infinitely preferable to a richer one disfigured by grab and competition.

As capitalism tends to increase self-interest, so would socialism tend to diminish it. I do not say more for it than that : but that, in all conscience, is enough. It is a myth that any system of organising society can of itself make men, to put it I suppose childishly, good. They can be made good only by religion, and you can understand the word as broadly or as narrowly as you like. But what socialism—real socialism—would do would be to obliterate some of the forces which at present deliberately strengthen the evil elements in men's nature. When it has done that, it has done everything which any sensible person could ask of it.

So far, indeed, am I from deprecating socialism when I insist on liberal values that, on the contrary, I regard the slow and compromising approach to socialism in the West as having been the main barrier to the fuller realisation of those values. We have been late in understanding that you can't keep life in watertight compartments, and that however much you may try to respect personality in one sector you can succeed only to a limited degree if your economic system is based on greed, which is inconsistent with that respect : to say nothing of the fact that devotion to a set of values can hardly be considered absolute if they are ruled out from the whole economic area of daily life. These considerations, always important, became a matter of spiritual life or death when the earlier capitalism took on its later monopoly form. Something can be said, though not as much as usually *is* said, for capitalism in its heyday : for all its essential wickedness and the horrible misery of its working-class victims, it was gay, it was adventurous, it was expansionist, and it could still its conscience, if it had one, with the reflection that it was adding to the total amount of wealth in the world, and so eventually to the ease and comfort of everyone. But capitalism in its monopoly phase has been nothing but a dull, dead mass of restrictionist greed. It is no accident that the rapid decay of general moral standards has synchronised with the last period of monopoly capitalism.

It must be added, however, no less emphatically that there is little merit in socialism as a matter of pure economics. Nationalisation and all the rest of it is so much mere machinery, though essential machinery; the aim is, or should be, the enhancement of personality. A technically socialist state, in the economic sense, can be as illiberal, as materialistic, as inhumane as a capitalist one: indeed, it can be more so. In other words, socialism is valuable only in so far as it serves our western values. That is why, in the following pages, I often prefer to use the broader words "liberal" and "liberalism" rather than the narrower ones "socialist" or "socialism". But because in the world of today liberalism can preserve itself only by flowering into socialism, the reader will understand that by liberalism I mean a liberal and humanistic socialism, wherever the context permits.

It is the fact that we are socialists in the sense I have tried to indicate that makes so many of us highly critical of the Labour Government. We "support" it, of course; for what would have been, or as things are could be, the alternative? Nothing but an attempt to maintain privilege, to bolster up monopoly capitalism, and to produce from the morgue of history the economic carcase of the past. (Which is not to deny that some Conservatives, and many Liberals, are far more enlightened than some Labour leaders who call themselves socialists and are certainly nationalisers.)

The present Government, on the other hand, is genuinely endeavouring in face of the most formidable difficulties to serve the material interests of the common people of Britain. That is a very great deal: but in the crisis we face it is not nearly enough. For the first charge against the Government must be that even in the domestic sphere its socialism is very partial: if it is cautiously socialist in economics, it is still almost wholly capitalist in its choice of incentives. Its general tone is materialistic, lacking in any appeal to altruistic motives, far too suggestive, not to put too fine a point on it, of bribery. But the second charge is still more important, and it is this : that the Government is failing or very largely failing to put into practice, and even into speech, the belief that national "interests" must always be over-ridden by considerations of the international good. For this, to say the truth, is in the main a national socialist Government ; and it is in power just at the time when respect for personality—that respect for the personality of all men everywhere which, as we have seen, is the essence of our civilisation—demands an inter-national socialism wholeheartedly accepted and consistently applied.

When Senator Vandenberg announced in the Senate his "re-luctant but firm conviction" that the proposed loan to Britain would "contribute to the continued well-being of the American people," and added that it was only on the basis of "intelligent American self-interest that the credit could be defended", he seemed not merely a typical but even a symbolic figure : for to suggest to capitalist America that the deliberate pursuit of self-interest, by a nation as a nation, is always unintelligent as well as immoral would be to qualify for incarceration with the criminally insane. But are our own language and our own practice so very different? I say nothing of the Press, which, with a few excep-tions, does more than merely assume that national self-interest should be the touchstone of policy : it explicitly says so, and I could give literally hundreds of examples to prove it. It is not, however, of journalists but of British labour politicians that I am thinking ; they too speak far more often and far more con-vincingly in a national than in an international spirit. "Industrial Britain" said Mr. Herbert Morrison on March 25th 1946 "set out to win prosperity for its people led by a Government with a programme to bring certain basic industries and services under Government ownership. . . . We were able, if we would, to tackle our industrial problems in a spirit and with a drive superior to any other country in the world. . . . We started our drive with an impetus that was surely irresistible. . . . We could, if we would, raise our standard of living to a height never before enjoyed by the bulk of our people." In the very next column of *The Times* the Prime Minister was reported as speaking on "the drive for export" in similar terms, if with the less vigorous phrasing that he prefers. Everyone knows, of course, that a large volume of exports is essential for this country, especially in the conditions of today : but is it so difficult to set the problem in a wider context, and must we so repeatedly talk in the language of economic chauvinism? Sometimes all limits are overstepped. "Imperial Chemical Industries" said the B.B.C. on May 3rd 1946 "have announced that work is to begin at once on a £9,000,000 expansion of their dyestuffs interests. . . . The expansion will, most of all, help Britain to capture much of those foreign markets which used to be dominated by German dyestuffs." As I listened I was nagged by a sense of familiarity: what dead voice was this that echoed from the past, and why was I suddenly terrified by the fear that for all the sharpness of our brains we men, the perverse and hard of heart, could never escape our doom? Then I remembered. "The truth is" said Mr. Lloyd George to Lord Riddell at Versailles "that we have got our way. We have got most of the things we set out to get. . . . The German navy has been handed over, the German merchant shipping has been handed over, and the German colonies have been given up. One of our chief trade competitors has been seriously crippled. . . ." That was good enough for the hard-faced men of 1919: is it good enough for the socialists of 1946?

I am not suggesting that the Labour Government is doing worse in such matters than a Conservative Government would have done: on the contrary, I am quite certain that it is doing far better. Nor do I wish to paint too black a picture: on May Day this year, for instance—an appropriate occasion for internationalist sentiments, but only a couple of days after the B.B.C. announcement just referred to—Mr. Attlee made a very fine speech, if I may be allowed to say so, in the true Keir Hardie tradition, and his Indian and Egyptian policies, to take only two examples, are as enlightened as anyone could desire. Indeed, his Indian policy, and the statement explaining it, will rank among the very greatest achievements in British history. But what really tells is the general tone of Government language as a whole and over a period, and above all the actual policies pursued when there is an obvious clash between immediate self-interest and the well-being of others: and in both respects the Government must be said very largely to have failed, even when full consideration has been given to the fact that they are "up against" the actions of others as well as of previous Governments in this country. Last winter a petition was presented to Mr. Attlee, signed by seven or eight hundred of the most eminent and representative people in the country, begging that the general rations here should not be raised so long as there was distress on the Continent of

Europe. "It would not be possible" said the Prime Minister in his letter of refusal "for any Government to make the standard of life of its people dependent on conditions, however brought about, in countries over which they have no control." Hating to criticise the leader of my party, I yet cannot find in that sentence any trace of a socialist accent, as I at least understand socialism. Indeed, if communism and the growing power of the Soviet Union are the strongest positive forces opposed to the stability and development of western civilisation, one of the strongest negative forces is the preoccupation of British Labour with domestic economics.

* * * *

I shall come now as quickly as possible to communism, to the Soviet Union and to Germany. But first I want to give some examples of dangerous tendencies on the Continent of Europe and in Great Britain—apart from this cult of self-interest, with which many of these tendencies are themselves "tied up"—that are not directly or certainly not wholly due to communist influence. The communists and elements on the extreme right are, it is true, foremost in displaying these tendencies : but the tendencies themselves are simply manifestations of that general decay of western values which is giving both communism and the extreme right, with their widely differing motives, a common opportunity. I shall speak of Britain first.

§ 1

In August 1945 the B.B.C. broadcast a talk about conditions then prevailing in German hospitals. Its picture of misery and pain must have horrified anyone whose sympathy with human suffering was not rigidly confined to what he could see with his own eyes or what was happening on his own doorstep. After finishing his description, the broadcaster added that his object was not to arouse pity for our late enemies, but to point out the inexpediency of permitting the development of epidemics "anywhere where there are Allied troops". Eight months later Field-marshal Viscount Montgomery, in the speech at Hastings from which I have already quoted, said that he also had been gravely concerned about the possibility of a serious epidemic in Germany—his anxiety however being that, if it spread to this country, we might not be "in a sufficiently good state after the war to stand up to it." About the same time his deputy, Lieutenant-General Sir Brian Robertson, was giving a Press conference in Berlin; rations in the British zone of Germany had just been cut to a level described by Sir Jack Drummond, Scientific Adviser to the Ministry of Food, as "starvation", and Sir Brian was warning his hearers that a still further reduction might be necessary. "Although Britain considered that the Germans should be adequately fed," he stated, "it was not because she was sorry for them but because it was a matter of policy." Well, I *am* sorry for them : I am sorry for every man, woman or child who is in pain and distress, including Joyce and Amery before their execution and the man Kramer of Belsen whose face was pilloried in almost every newspaper for the baser public to make a mock of. Indeed, I am sorriest of all for people like Kramer, since there is more, there are spiritual things as well as physical, for which to pity them. This deprecation of mercy and pity, this denial of the gentleness which is the distinguishing mark of Judaeo-Christian liberalism, is becoming, indeed, a positive mania : there is hardly a politician, hardly a newspaper whether of the study or of the gutter, that doesn't succumb to it. I would go further, and say that if you were to believe our public men you would think that pity and mercy were not merely irrelevant but positively disgraceful, and that to have nothing whatever to do with them was a basic ethical duty. So pervasive is this new morality that even men who are obviously moved largely or even solely by humanitarian considerations pay lip-service to it, and hurriedly add, when they mention pity, "That, of course, is not the primary consideration". They appear to be afraid that otherwise people might think them wicked.

I have given only three examples, but I have in front of me a file of newspaper cuttings that would fill a volume much bigger than this. Yet the overwhelming majority of Englishmen and Englishwomen are not in the least, I am convinced, what politicians and the baser Press would lead you to suppose : they still believe in their hearts, whatever may be the appearances to the contrary, that if they speak with the tongues of men and of angels, but have not love, they are become sounding brass or clanging cymbals. The danger, for all that, is pressing ; for if from laziness or cowardice or whatever it may be we fail to check this growing degradation, we are condemning our children to a norm, which we are ourselves helping to establish, of recog-

23

nised and respectable immorality. Cannot we then put away childish things, and not merely refuse to join in this chorus but openly protest against it? Cannot we say quite plainly that we hate the idea of epidemics in Germany not because, as you will hear day after day, "the Channel is no barrier against germs", but because epidemics are a horror to the people, whoever they may be, who suffer them? Must we hide the fact—and the very question is a measure of our moral collapse—that we want to feed starving Germans not primarily as a matter of policy, but primarily because starvation is intrinsically abominable? Must we, in a word, continue to pretend that we are worse than we are?

Even viler, perhaps, than the explicit rejection of pity, which at any rate implies that the thing rejected has some claim to consideration, is the attitude of callous ferocity and self-righteous contempt, an attitude not even studied but worn quite casually and as a matter of course, which many of our most popular journalists adopt towards anyone generally regarded as disreputable or an enemy. Pity (which of course need not qualify to the smallest degree the genuine sort of justice) simply does not enter into their calculations. I have already mentioned Joyce and Kramer and Amery: I will give only a few more examples, and then leave it to the reader to fill out the list for himself from his own recollection of his newspaper reading during the last few months. The examples I choose are no more outrageous than many others that will immediately come to mind.

Some months ago a British newspaper, and I have no doubt several others, displayed a huge front-page photograph of the dead Mussolini by the side of his dead lover, on show in a street of Milan. Italians had taken the bodies after execution and strung them up by the heels, and were now dishonouring them. They had forgotten that death, the leveller, wipes away all human distinctions, all gradations of good or evil, right or wrong: dead men are either spirits, which is awful, or nothing, which is more awful still. Feeling this awe, decent people raise their hats, or incline their heads, when death passes by. Italians may be excused for forgetting this and kicking the dead flesh in the heat of passion: British journalists, or the masters they were obeying, kicked it coldly and vicariously, and earned their daily bread by blaspheming.

Pierre Laval was tried, if that is the just word—not that any-one would deny for a moment that he was guilty of betraying

France to fascism—and condemned to death. On the morning of execution he attempted to commit suicide, and nearly succeeded. The doctors fought for his life and saved it : then, very weak but fully conscious, he was carried to the firing squad. I do not blame the French for this act of detestable cruelty, which was clearly motivated, not by a sense of justice, for his death from the poison would have satisfied that, but by a craving for vengeance, which could be content with nothing less than the maximum agony. No, I do not blame the French, for many of them had suffered more horribly than we can find it easy to imagine under the Vichy régime. But what is to be said of the newspapers in our own country which made this disgusting scene front-page and head-line news : which spared us no detail of Laval's double agony : which titillated our sadism, and flattered our sense of moral superiority, by exhibiting a fellow human being in the torments of hell? That sort of malpractice, consistently indulged in, must coarsen and brutalize a people against whose hearts and minds it is committed.

The third example is also from France. There was a picture in the newspapers shortly after the liberation of that country. It showed a woman with a baby in her arms. Her head was shaved, so that she no longer looked like a woman ; and she was running the gauntlet down a double row of people, who were jeering and pointing fingers. She had slept, I suppose, with a German or collaborationist, and this pillorying of motherhood, which ought in all circumstances to be sacred, was the primitive reaction of a war-tortured populace. Again, I do not blame the French : but again I ask, what is to be thought of newspapers which served up this spectacle for the edification of our own people at their Christian breakfast tables ? Quite a number of them, no doubt, were to read the following Sunday about Christ writing on the ground, and telling those who were without sin to cast the first stone at the woman taken in adultery.

Spiritual and sometimes physical pornography in pictorial form is indeed becoming the mode. One newspaper was not content with a mere verbal description of Laval's agony : for the benefit of those unable or unwilling to read, a vivid picture of the scene was sprawled across the top of the front page. This was the caption : "It is 12.30 p.m., a minute to go for the hour of Pierre Laval. He stands to the right of the picture, dressed in black, hands tied behind his back. To the left the firing party awaits the order. . . ." At about the same time there was a

25

photograph of the wretched girl Grese with a great figure 9 on her bosom. Above it were the words "No 9—Guilty," and below it "When a child she wept if her kitten was teased." A pagan in Rome might have murmured *Sunt lacrimae rerum* at thought of what those words implied, and put the photograph away: but a twentieth-century Englishman was not so sensitive. In another newspaper, under the heading "Weighed by Order," you could see a woman on the scales, and others waiting their turn. "British field ambulance men" said the underline "weighing German adults in a Berlin street . . . to discover the lowest basis for rationing to ensure fitness for work without causing malnutrition." The less stupid Legrees did the same. And the communist *Daily Worker* was not to be outdone in this competition for "toughness". These were the words below a picture in its issue of December 28th, 1945: "Franz Strasser, condemned to die for the murder of two American airmen after a forced landing, hears the accusation read as he waits for the drop to fall".

The final example is perhaps, in its cold wickedness, the worst of all. "All around Potsdam," said the B.B.C. spokesman last summer, describing the conference of the "Big Three," "German families are living on a diet largely of potatoes and irregular bread." That was the time when the misery in Berlin was nearing its climax: the city was riddled with death, starvation and disease. The B.B.C. spokesman continued, however, with no hint of disapproval, in the following terms: "But within the heavily guarded compound provided for the American delegation there are two ten-ton mobile refrigerators and they are full of the best cuts of meat. This with fresh fruit, strawberries, melons, tomatoes and hearts of lettuce, will be served today and henceforth. Two dieticians are watching the balance of calories and vitamins. Ice is being brought in from Berlin to cool the drinks, and those drinks will include every kind of wine and spirits and liqueurs. Supply convoys have brought in stoves for cooking and the American Air Force flew in twenty refrigerators from Great Britain. In addition, there's an astonishing list of requirements for the comfort of the delegates, including, as a brief sample, five hundred mosquito nets, five thousand linen sheets, a hundred and fifty bottles of button polish, five hundred corkscrews and bottle-openers, and one thousand white coats for waiters. American engineers have been carrying out major building conversions in the American compound, including the erection of brand new houses, the conversion of German houses into restaurants, and the laying and the clearing-up of the gardens. Potsdam was knocked about by Allied bombing and fighting: it's now become one of the most gleaming, spotless, luxurious garden suburbs in the world." A fitting prelude, indeed, this vaunting of the contrast between the starvation and misery of some and the soft luxury of others, to the news of the dictate from Potsdam that will bedevil the world for generations and perhaps for centuries.

But this, it may be said, was after all nearly a year ago, when the passions of war were still raging. Well, as I pass these proofs for press Mr. Herbert Morrison has just been broadcasting to the American people about famine in Europe. "We do not love the Germans," he said, "but their coal, which they cannot mine if they are starving, is vital to the economic reconstruction of Europe." That is slavers' language. If anybody thinks I exaggerate, this can only be because our growing insensitiveness has escaped our own attention.

*　　*　　*　　*

If pity and mercy are inseparable from the Christianity or liberal humanism in which we profess to believe, so no less is some degree of personal and national humility, some attempt at least to modify the complacent self-righteousness that comes so easily to almost every one of us. In our relation with the Germans have we made the slightest attempt, either during the war or since, to modify this self-righteousness? Have we not rather, nearly all of us, given it the freest possible play, enjoyed it and luxuriated in it to the full? I could deal, if I had the space, with the outcry that deafened us at the time of the Buchenwald "revelations", which were no revelation at all to those who had been trying ever since 1933 to rouse a lazy and sceptical public and to speak for men and women who, shut away from the world and without voices of their own, were suffering unspeakable torments in those camps of iniquity. Now at last we knew, people said, that the whole German nation was guilty: if not, why didn't they protest against these outrages and revolt against Hitler, no matter what the cost? It did not occur to them to ask what they would have done in similar circumstances: they did not pause to wonder whether, when the cost of which they talked so glibly would have been death or torture not for themselves alone but for their children also, they would have been, without any possibility of doubt, sufficiently heroic to run the risk of it. They did not even ask themselves why, so long as we were still at peace, Buchenwald had been no concern of theirs, even though to raise their voices in protest would have meant not death or torture or even the risk of imprisonment, but the loss of a few seconds of time and the expenditure of some negligible fraction of energy. Instead of asking themselves things like that, they preferred to luxuriate in the sense of their own immense superiority.

But I wish to speak, not of that, but of what is called, in the current jargon, "re-education." The very word is detestable, so instinct is it, as commonly employed, with an odious pharisaism. I must not be taken to imply that re-education, properly understood, is unnecessary or unimportant: on the contrary, it is more important than almost anything else in European politics today. Nor do I deny that there are many sincere and honourable people who are devoting their time and energy, in complete selflessness, to the work of eradicating the legacy of Hitlerism. What I mean is that the mental and spiritual approach of the overwhelming majority—and I am speaking of decent people, not of those who cry out for vengeance—is utterly lacking in the instinctive humility which alone could give promise of success. "We, being without sin," is what we are saying "will graciously teach you, very gradually we are afraid, to become a decent people—in fact, to become in the end perhaps almost as good as ourselves." What we should be saying, if our attitude were dictated by humility and respect for personality, would be something, on the contrary, like this: "We have all sinned, and no one of us can cast stones. We in Britain have had a fortunate history, which has enabled us to win a large measure of freedom and democracy. Your history, on the other hand, has been unfortunate: when you have tried to advance to freedom and democracy circumstances have thwarted you, and the thwarting has weakened you in independence and civic courage—which is not to deny that there has been a magnificent minority that has stood firm against fearful odds. Finally, very evil men, God forgive them, have got control over you, and have committed in your name, and have led some of you to commit, unspeakable wickedness. You are now stricken to the dust, and we feel for you as members of our common human brotherhood. We hold out a helping hand: accept it, please, and take from our history and our way of life anything that may seem good and useful to you." Isn't that, or something like it, the attitude most likely to touch the hearts and influence the minds of our late enemies? I might also mention, if this were the place, the element of hypocrisy in our whole procedure: for to starve the Germans, and to do to them some of the very things which Hitler did to others, seems an odd background for re-education. There is really only one way to re-educate people, and that is by force of example. You may properly describe, in addition, what liberalism and democracy in your opinion mean: but if you once attempt to inculcate these things, you merely prove by doing so that you are ignorant yourself of their true nature. And what in any case is wanted far more than the re-education of one people by another is the repentance of all peoples everywhere.

* * * *

We have been considering certain qualities of men and women —pity, mercy, humility—which are being progressively weakened in the Britain of today. But there is also an institution which is suffering attacks; and because it is the very bastion of our western values, because its integral maintenance is the ultimate test of our respect for personality, we must resist to the uttermost all attempts to sap it, unimportant and unsuccessful though they so far may have been. The institution is freedom of speech; and the attacks on it are being made, by a horrible paradox, in the name of antifascism, which should be its most fanatical defender.

Fanatical, indeed, is not too strong a word. Fanaticism in general is no doubt to be deprecated, for it implies an absence of tolerance; but if there is one thing about which we have a positive duty to be fanatical it must surely be freedom of speech. The four freedoms have been, theoretically at least, the mode ever since President Roosevelt enunciated them; but the truth is that only one of them is fundamental. With freedom of speech, every other freedom is at any rate possible; without it, all are in jeopardy. To say that freedom of speech means the freedom of Press barons, or the freedom to hire a hall if you have enough money, and other half-truths of the kind, is no doubt all very well on a party platform; but let a man who talks like that find himself overnight in a police State, where dangerous thoughts are the passport for gaol when not for something worse, and he will very quickly change his tune. If freedom of speech were ever to be seriously threatened in this country all other political issues would immediately become devoid of any importance whatsoever: socialists and capitalists, Christians and atheists, Jews and antisemites would have to drop all the differences and hostilities that otherwise divide them, and unite in defence of the only thing that now really mattered.

We got through the war with a degree of free expression which will be to our eternal credit, and which would have been quite impossible for any people whose instinct for it was less deep-seated than ours. We were allowed to say just what we liked provided only that we didn't damage the war effort, and sometimes even when, on a maliciously narrow interpretation, it might have been held that we did. Throughout the whole course of the war I did not submit a single manuscript to the Ministry of Information except when some question of military secrets might be involved, and though many books I published were highly critical of Government policy there was never so much as a hint of official disapproval. Every other publisher, I believe, could say the same. By war-time standards, Mr. Herbert Morrison was particularly liberal in his treatment both of fascists and of communists. He refrained from suppressing *The Daily Worker,* during its defeatist phase, until its sabotage of the war effort had become positively dangerous: he let Mosley out directly he felt able, and was undeterred by a campaign of intolerence half hysterical and half engineered. Blots of course there have been, both during the war and since, and notably the deplorable Sansom case; but they have been surprisingly and honourably few.

With this record behind us, are we going, a year after the war is over, to listen to people who would tamper with the most sacred of our institutions? The cry is to "outlaw fascism and antisemitism": or, to put it plainly, to make the expression of fascist and antisemitic opinions illegal and liable to punishment. Communists are taking the lead, and the National Council for Civil Liberties has recently made nonsense of its name and objects by supporting the demand; but many non-communists of the left, and some, I regret to say, of my fellow Jews, are joining in the clamour. The Government, supported by all liberal opinion, by every socialist who understands what socialism means, by the general body of conservatives, and of course by the extreme right (whose motives are suspect) have shown no signs of yielding; but the pressure continues, and will certainly grow stronger with every new incident, however trivial, of fascist or antisemitic activity.

If you tell these people that freedom of speech means freedom of speech, and not freedom to say only what the majority consider it wise or decent or expedient or moral to say, they parry you with a reply which, I notice, was recently employed by Stalin himself in a slightly different form and in another connection. "Free speech" they say "must not be used for the purpose of suppressing free speech." They mean that if fascists are allowed to express their opinions you will get fascism, and what about freedom then? It might be objected that to imagine democracy as feeble as all that is neither very sensible nor very patriotic; or again that, what is sauce for the gander being sauce for the goose, communist opinion might very well be suppressed for the same reason. But there is only one objection that really matters, and it is this: that if you silence fascists for fear that fascism will be established, you have already half established it by the very fact of silencing them.

Is it really necessary to state all over again the case for freedom of expression as Mill and Voltaire stated it, or to fight once more, two centuries later, the battle of the Enlightenment? Apparently it is. Lacking the ability, I will put the matter in a perhaps childishly religious way, which can be understood either literally or metaphorically according to taste—as follows: I am certain that my opinion is right and yours is wrong: you are certain that yours is right and mine is wrong: but only God can really *know* which is right and which is wrong, or, to be more exact, what degree of rightness there is in either. By suppressing opinion, therefore—any opinion, however obviously abominable it may appear—I am assuming God's prerogative of knowledge and judgment, and am perhaps in consequence murdering truth. Every man may be, and in some degree must be, an instrument for the communication of truth: there are no instruments but men: to silence a single voice is therefore to interfere with the communication. There is the argument as I learned it at my mother's knee, and fifty years or so later I can see no flaw in it. People who object to bringing God into the matter can think in terms of history instead.

To abandon your belief in the sacredness of this freedom at the very point where it means something—at the point where the opinions to be expressed seem horrible to you—is to convict yourself either of muddle-headedness or of hypocrisy. I happen to regard fascism as an utter abomination, as almost the final wickedness of which men are capable; but I am driven to paraphrase Voltaire as he has been paraphrased a million times before, and to say that while I detest fascism I will nevertheless fight to the death for the right of fascists to express their opinions.

It will be objected, I am sure, that this sort of thing is all very well theoretically, but that in practice the question is one of weighing risks. Perhaps there is a risk, people will say, that by suppressing fascist opinions you are weakening the principle of free expression; but by not suppressing them you are running the far greater risk of making fascism, which is the enemy of all freedom, a reality. Such an argument, I reply, ignores the continuity of the historical process, fails to understand the facts of human nature, and thinks statically instead of dynamically. Fascism is not some separate and isolated phenomenon, which can magically be brought into existence by appealing to people's reason or playing on their prejudices: it is the logical development of certain traits that are in the human nature of all of us. If you strengthen these traits you make fascism more probable: if you strengthen the opposing ones you make it less so. The strongest of all the antifascist traits is the passion for spiritual and intellectual freedom; and by so much as you restrict its play, by so much as you nourish instead the sado-masochistic elements in our nature, by so much as you introduce the first thin wedge of authoritarianism, by just so much do you bring a little nearer the very peril you are anxious to avoid.

If even that is too theoretical for people who imagine that theory and practice occupy watertight compartments, consider probabilities in a manner that even they can understand. Every act of suppression drives underground, inflames passions, makes martyrs, inflates trifles, dignifies absurdities, and produces just the publicity that every mischief-maker desires. Suppress enough people long enough, and you get that atmosphere of civic strife from which every kind of ruthlessness and authoritarianism derives its natural sustenance. The common-sense way of dealing with fascist propaganda is to ignore it, to remove the grievances that offer it its chance, and to give the widest possible scope to every liberty-loving instinct in the community. When the Home Secretary said something of this kind recently in the House of Commons, a member or two, if I remember rightly, objected that German experience refuted him.

On the contrary, it proved his case right up to the hilt. Hitler came to power in an atmosphere of civic violence, at a time of appalling insecurity and unemployment, and in a country where democracy had never had any real opportunity of establishing itself in the thoughts and institutions of the populace.

What applies to fascist applies also to antisemitic propaganda. I am sometimes asked by my fellow Jews whether I would see another six million of us massacred sooner than give way on a point of punctilio. The short answer is that to suppress opinion, whether antisemitic or otherwise, is precisely to produce the sort of world in which another six million Jews *will* be massacred. Let antisemites say as often and as loudly as they like that we are greedy, or dishonest, or just vaguely a menace to the happiness of the world : we can refute them, not by forbidding them to say it, but by showing them in practice that this is exactly what we are not. For Jews, indeed, to acquiesce in, or still worse to demand, the suppression of antisemitic opinion would be to submit to a gross indignity which no one with a scrap of pride could tolerate.

The question of community libel is on a different footing. If legislation could be devised, hedged about with every possible safeguard, and designed to penalize not expressions of opinion but provable mis-statements of fact, then I think it might be salutary. Antisemites have as much right to say that Judaism is obnoxious as I have to say the same of capitalism ; but if they choose to write that Jews are required to kill Christian babies, or that the Protocols of Zion is an authentic document of Jewish provenance, then if the contrary can be proved by the ordinary rules of evidence they ought perhaps to be punished, the punishment being heavier on presumption of malice and lighter on proof of feeble-mindedness, and in any event as moderate as possible. By the same token, I ought perhaps to be punished if I wrote that capitalism inevitably involves the personal dishonesty of every capitalist, including myself. I confess, however, that I am not very keen about all this, for the dangers might very well outrun the advantages.

But this question of community libel is a minor point. The important thing is to stand firm on the broad issue of free expression, and not only of that but of civil liberties in general, and of the large tolerance that is basic in our tradition. The American leader of a curious religious sect, with a number of adherents in this country, was recently permitted to come here on a two months' visit. He preaches, it is understood, "absolute honesty." The antifascist stalwarts at once protested against his entry, not, I am sure, because of his creed, but on the ground that (in common with some well-known British politicians) he had once praised the Nazis. The incident, which was not an isolated one, might seem too trivial for mention ; but that kind of inverted fascism can spread very rapidly in the present climate unless we are careful. And is it realised that this island may soon be left almost alone as a guardian of civil liberties? The Hungarian National Assembly recently passed a bill "for the defence of the democratic Constitution and the Republic." This makes it a criminal offence to publish facts, *whether true or untrue*, " apt to cause contempt for the democratic Constitution or the Republic or to impair international esteem for the country." Only a historian could say whether there is any precedent in the whole history of European civilisation for quite so explicit a blasphemy. Still, Hungary is a "far-off country of which we know little." But France is nearer. The proposed French Constitution, which was the subject of a referendum in May, provided that if the Republic were declared by the Assembly to be in danger, freedom of movement and assembly, the liberty of the press and the secrecy of correspondence might be abolished by a two-thirds majority. The Constitution was narrowly rejected ; and though this was a defeat for the socialists as well as for the communists, and though it is in the socialists that I rest all my hopes for the future of France, I for one am very glad indeed that it was.

* * * *

Finally, and still speaking of our own country, I come to what may be called respect for truth, or the Socratic spirit, or intellectual integrity, or a determination to follow the argument whither it may lead. This essential element in our civilisation has never been particularly strong : it was decaying rapidly in the late thirties : but the pace is now accelerating, even among educated people, to a quite disastrous degree.

The specifically communist form of the disease will be considered in a later section. A good deal, too, will be said about the way in which the less responsible Press misuses its power, and commits the malpractice of fitting the facts to the argument instead of the argument to the facts. Meanwhile, one exhibit may be worth many pages of description. These were the headlines in certain popular newspapers on the morning of February 27th 1946:

"400,000 Given Homes Since War's End."—*Daily Mirror*.
"Homes Found Already for 400,000."—*Daily Herald*.
"16,220 Completed, 47,398 Being Built."—*News Chronicle*.
"Only 16,220 Houses are Completed."—*Daily Worker*.
"1,909 Homes."—*Daily Mail*.
"Bevan Boys Build 350 Houses So Far."—*Daily Express*.

* * * *

But it is in the use of words, not to express more or less clear ideas, but as stimuli for arousing emotions which are always unreasoning and usually base, that the decay of the Socratic spirit is most clearly to be seen. Here are three examples, taken almost at random from what could and can be heard at any time on the various political platforms:

(1) *"Fascist"* or *"Trotskyite"*. Anyone who supports the Soviet Union in all its policies uses these words to discredit anyone else, whether humanitarian or Christian or pacifist or Liberal or Labour, who doesn't.

(2) *" The Communist Menace"*. This is a phrase used by die-hard Tories to frighten people into believing that something vaguely horrible will happen to them under any form of socialism.

(3) *"The freedom of the unemployed is the freedom to starve"*. I must have heard this at dozens of Labour Party meetings during the General Election. The word "freedom" is deliberately used in two different senses. The object is to arouse anticapitalist emotions, and to suggest that any freedom the working class may have in a " bourgeois democracy " is comparatively worthless, if indeed not entirely bogus.

There is another group of expressions which you will find in the speeches of the very great, particularly Stalin's, in numerous State papers, and above all in those joint pronunciamenti by the Big Three to which Mr. Churchill or whoever may happen to be the British member of the trio for the time being is happy to lend his name. The commonest of them are "the peace-loving nations" and "the freedom-loving nations." You would think that the Almighty had fixed, once and for all, certain categories of humanity, to say nothing of the enigma that a country which changes sides is an aggressor one day and peace-loving the next. These idiot phrases are, of course, almost literally meaningless.

35

The most bloodthirsty and tyrannical of politicians has only to oppose the common enemy, and he qualifies overnight as a lover of freedom and peace. I say " politicians ", because there is this further stupidity in these expressions, over and above their other shortcomings, that they personalize non-existent abstractions.

The most abused of all words is " democracy ". The Soviet Union employs it, half or perhaps quite genuinely, in a sense entirely different from our own. But there is nothing genuine at all about its use in this country by the extreme left on the one hand and by almost the whole of the right on the other. The left calls you antidemocratic (not to say fascist) if you criticise any policy, however antidemocratic, of the Soviet Union ; and the right calls you antidemocratic if you seek so much as to nibble at monopoly capitalism, and to prevent it, in however limited a degree, from exploiting the community. All that is really meant in both cases is that you are saying or doing something which is not to the taste of the politicians in question.

With the combination " economic democracy " a further stage of dishonesty or muddle is reached. It is almost common form nowadays to say that Russia has economic democracy, and we have political democracy, and somehow or other we must combine their merits. Now " economic democracy " is a very difficult concept. I was a Guild Socialist forty years ago, and I well remember our discussions of this question, which was our primary concern. We held as a matter of course that economic democracy could mean only one thing, namely the direct control of an industry by the workers engaged in it : the sole problem being how that control could be achieved. There is certainly no economic democracy of this kind in the Soviet Union. Others consider that a country is economically democratic if the incomes of all its inhabitants are approximately equal. But in the Soviet Union the disparity of incomes (though not of wealth) is certainly as great as in many if not all of the capitalist countries, and perhaps greater than in some. There may be a sense in which the Soviet Union is an economic democracy, but people who use the phrase so easily certainly don't know what it is. What they really mean is that Russia has abolished private capitalism, which is something entirely different.

These few examples of verbal black magic must suffice : a week's conversation or newspaper reading will provide a crop of others. But if I have dealt with this topic briefly, that is not because it is unimportant. Indeed, from one point of view

36

it is the most important of all. What is truth? was asked at the great turning-point of western history. Deliberate lying, the answer might have been, is mental aggression in its most abominable form : it is as much an outrage against the minds of others as deliberate starvation is an outrage against their bodies. For could anything be worse than an act of power that with wilful intent shuts out the innocent from all contact with reality ? So far, lying in this country has been in the main more casual than deliberate ; but elsewhere the light of truth is being increasingly put out of set purpose, and more and more men are being placed at the intellectual disposal of others. In the name, then, of an overwhelming responsibility let every one of us turn his back on the smallest temptation to speak less than the truth in however noble a cause—I say every one of us, for I certainly have no wish to plead not guilty—and remember that Socrates was as much a founder of our civilisation in his own way as were Moses and Christ in theirs.

§ 2

On the Continent of Europe there are three developments—still apart from the major question of communism and the Soviet Union—which are turning our civilisation backward in its course. They are the normalization of resistance traits, the intensification of nationalism often in its crudest racial form, and a reversion to a more barbaric concept of justice.

A great deal of sentimental nonsense is talked about the resistance, and this must be said at the risk of being charged with ingratitude and ungenerosity. Among the resisters in various countries there were many men and women and even children of a large-hearted nobility, of a selfless devotion, and of an almost incredible courage that can evoke nothing but humility in any-one who remembers what they did and what they suffered. There were also many rogues and adventurers, and others who, because they were violent or deceitful by nature, found in these movements a suitable opportunity for activities that were palat-able to them. But the point is not so much what types of men they were who joined these movements, but what were the quali-ties that were necessarily developed under stress of them. These qualities were violence, sabotage, deceit, and a preference for adventurous excitement to steady work of a less romantic nature. This is not said by way of criticism : even if other means might have been possible (and such means were adopted to some extent, notably in Norway) it was hardly to be avoided that, in the present stage of human development, and for people immediately subject to the passions of war and invasion, the evil should, on the whole, be fought by methods which were themselves intrinsically evil. But the result must be faced. If a man, year after year, is violent and even cruel as a matter of right, he finds it difficult to become gentle when the occasion for violence is past : if to deceive the enemy is his highest duty, he becomes addicted to deceit : if excitement and adventure have been meat and drink to him, steady routine work is boring daily fare. So far as violence is concerned, it might be objected that what applies to the resistance must apply also to the soldiers and sailors and airmen of all countries who fought their respective enemies. So to a certain extent it does, but not to the same extent. Most serving men looked upon their job as something necessary but unpleasant and exceptional, which they would be only too happy to abandon as soon as they could : and this constant sense that they were acting against their nature modified the effect which the practice of violence might otherwise have had. But in sections of the resistance violence and deceit and adventure rapidly assumed the aspect of normal daily life.

Moreover, it was the duty of all patriotic people under occupation, whether they were active resisters or not, to resist passively by ca' canny in every possible form. And the rhythm of hard work is something not easily reacquired.

It seems to me quite certain, from conversations with many people of judgment who have talked about conditions in their own countries, that in several parts of formerly occupied Europe characteristics of the resistance, active and passive, show signs of becoming almost the norm of daily behaviour. And these characteristics, which were in some degree, and relatively to the situation, virtues then, are plainly vices now.

In several of these countries considerable sections of the population, formerly industrious, now do as little work as they conveniently can. The search is for the easiest money, no matter how it may be obtained. Honesty, if not the exception, is certainly not the rule. Crimes, particularly of violence and against property, have increased alarmingly. Sexual ethics mean little, and the statistics of venereal disease are horrifying.

It would be quite untrue, of course, to suggest that all this is solely or even mainly due to the normalization, after the war, of characteristics typical of the resistance during the course of it. The food shortage, the economic dislocation, the demoralizing effects of enemy occupation, and most of all the ethical degradation of war itself, all play their part. Nor would it become the citizen of a country that has suffered so immeasurably less than these others to adopt an attitude of offensive superiority. But anyone who cares for European civilisation dare not shut his eyes to the facts: and these show, to my mind unquestionably, that respect for personality is weaker in Europe today than it has been at any period during my own lifetime. That imposes an immense responsibility on Britain, which, for all the criticisms that have been made, is in so much better a case.

* * * *

The second development on the Continent of Europe is the intensification of nationalism. Let us be perfectly clear that nationalism is a vice. By "nationalism" should be understood any undue consciousness of nationality, and if that seems to beg the whole question the reader will readily grasp what I mean. Nationalism is a vice because it concentrates on comparative inessentials—where a man lives, what sort of language he speaks, the type of his culture, the character of his "blood"—and ignores the essential, which is simply that he is a man. It pursues a spurious and abstract "national glory," which is devoid of any actual existence, and has nothing whatever to do with the glory, or with the daily and hourly happiness and well-being, of the nationals in question. It is partly an invention of ambitious and unscrupulous politicians, and partly a drug from which the populace derives, not individual peace of mind or the fulfilment of the genuine needs of their human nature, but a kind of bogus and vicarious satisfaction. It makes one set of people hate another set that they haven't the smallest real occasion for hating: it leads to jealousy, expansionism, oppression, strife, and eventually war.

I am sitting at a table by my window as I write this, looking over a country lane. It is Easter Day of 1946, and summer this year is already almost here. I am happy, in spite of what I am writing about, for two reasons: the warmth of the sun and the smell of the grass are beautiful, and I am engaged in an activity that fulfils the needs of my nature. Doesn't that make me kin to every man and woman in every country? Doesn't everybody want the same as I—enjoyment of the world and self-expression? What does it matter, in comparison with this, that I speak English and somebody else speaks German, that my skin is white and a Negro's black, that I am a Jew and my neighbour a Gentile? What does it matter that I live in Berkshire, but a second man near Budapest and a third man by the Rhine? What does it even matter that my "culture" is partly English and partly Jewish, while others have some other tradition that is the result not only of settled life in some particular region for a number of generations, but also of innumerable contacts between the various peoples of the world since the beginning of history? Let us, in the name of all reason and common-sense, forget these differences, and remember our common humanity.

That is not to imply that the preservation of a particular tradition is, even relatively, of no importance. On the contrary, we may rightly consider it, as I consider the preservation of our western tradition, of an importance difficult to exaggerate. But we go wrong the moment either we think of our tradition as a close preserve for men living in a particular area or born of a particular race, or we seek to impose it forciby on others. The thing to do with a tradition is to live it wholeheartedly, and to hope that others will come by contact with it to recognise its merits.

All this would simply not have been worth writing forty or even twenty-five years ago, for it would have been thought too obvious and commonplace. Of course there was nationalism then as there had previously so often been, and in many places it was rampant. But the general view among spiritually educated people was that it was something to be deprecated, a defect which somehow or other we must endeavour to eradicate. Now, the mood in Europe, very largely as an aftermath of Nazi practice, is all the other way. Nationalism is again something good, glorious, "sacro", something that it is unpatriotic or disreputable to denounce.

Of all forms of nationalism, racialist nationalism is the worst. Territorial or cultural nationalism at any rate corresponds to a fact: but racialist nationalism is wholly and perniciously unreal. What in Heaven's name can it signify, for the actual daily lives of men and women, whether they are of Slav or Teutonic or Magyar or Jewish or Aryan or no matter what sort of special race or special blood? Even if there were really anything "special" about it—even if the purity of races were not a childish and exploded legend—the unreality would still be complete; but the whole thing being mythical, the unreality is even greater, or would be if that were possible.

With the world as it is, certain instances of nationalism are no doubt necessary evils. Where a group, recognisable as a group, has been oppressed or ill-treated, or thinks it has been oppressed or ill-treated, by some other and more powerful group, usually in the name of the latter's national pride or egoism or glory, nationalism may be the only way out of an intolerable situation, and a necessary prelude to international harmony. Irish and Jewish nationalism are of this type. So are the "native" nationalisms now emerging everywhere, for they bear the marks, mixed up with other less desirable characteristics, of a genuine struggle for freedom from alien exploitation. But while all this is true, it should nevertheless be recognised that even in such cases the nationalism, though necessary, is an evil; and the evil can clearly be seen in the fact that such movements, originally defensive, only save themselves with difficulty from the development of those arrogant, exclusive, chauvinistic stigmata which are typically nationalist in the baser sense.

Glance round Europe today and ask yourselves whether, in these last few pages, I have exaggerated. I cannot load this essay, which I am anxious to keep as short as possible, with examples, and shall cite only one, namely that of Czechoslovakia. I have already written a good deal on this subject in the Press, and have been accused of some special hostility to the Czechoslovak people. This is absurd. I feel no hostility to any people, not even, if I must put it that way, to the Germans, in whose name six million of my fellow Jews were slaughtered. My bias is, in point of fact, well in the other direction. In 1939 I published G. E. R. Gedye's "Fallen Bastions", which will always be the classic denunciation of Hitler's attack on Czechoslovakia, and I made very special arrangements for its widest possible circulation. Later I published books by Dr. Ripka, now a leading Czechoslovak Minister, and several others. I am one of those who, not so many years ago, marched through the streets of London crying "Save Czechoslovakia! Save peace!" We thought of Czechoslovakia then as decent and tolerant—indeed, almost as the model of a liberal democracy. And now how is it all ending?

I shall speak later on, and in another connection, of the expulsion of Germans from their homes, not only in Czechoslovakia, but in Poland and East Prussia and Polish-occupied Germany and anywhere else where these unhappy people were to be found. I shall describe, in the words of eye-witnesses, the abominable cruelty with which these expulsions were, and are being, carried out. But I must anticipate for my present purpose, and remind the reader that, in spite of everything Dr. Beneš said during the earlier years of the war and when still in London, he had no sooner returned to his own country than he initiated or approved the wholesale expulsion of all but an insignificant minority of the Sudeten German population. The fact that a third of it—say a million in round figures—had stood firmly behind Dr. Beneš in the critical days before Munich,* and that its Labour movement had risked everything for its anti-Nazi convictions, was to count for nothing. The expulsions were for a time interrupted, as a result, to some extent, of public protests in this country; but the policy still stands, and it is likely that all these people will have been expelled from their homes by the end of the summer.

The plea of "security" by which this piece of abominable injustice was defended must be plainly characterized as to a high degree hypocritical. The evidence for this is indisputable. The policy was to apply, not only to Germans, but to Hungarians as well. In the new electoral law, published earlier this year, everyone who is not of "Slav nationality" is explicitly disfranchised; that is to say, not only Sudeten Germans and Hungarians but British wives of Czech nationals, and children of Jews who had described themselves as of Jewish nationality in a former census and whose families may have lived in Czechoslovakia for generations, are deprived of the fundamental right of democratic citizenship. There has been little attempt, either, to discriminate between the "guilty" and those who are demonstrably "innocent" or who may be "innocent" but cannot prove it; and "innocent Jews", sons of German-speaking citizens of Czechoslovakia who have meanwhile, perhaps, been gassed at Auschwitz, are being grossly penalised. The plain fact is that what lies behind this policy, and what contributed more to its adoption than any considerations of national security, was Dr. Beneš' desire that Czechoslovakia should be "free"—he has

---

* " . . . the anti-Nazi Sudeten Germans, who never numbered less than one-third of the whole." *Munich, Before and After*, by H. Ripka, p. 31. Gollancz, 1939.

used the word, but Hitler invented it—of anyone not blessed with Slavic "blood."

"Broadcasts from Czechoslovakia", wrote the Diplomatic Correspondent of *The Manchester Guardian* on June 5th 1945 " reflect a strong feeling of nationalism amounting almost to neo-Imperialism. In all current broadcasts the magnitude of the united Slav bloc comprising 200,000,000 European Slavs is emphasised ". He went on to quote the following from a declaration by Dr. Beneš' Minister of Education, a communist:

"Nothing but cultural debris surrounds us. We shall take our civilisation to the border regions. We shall plant there our national cultural ideals. Let us look at Central Europe. There are the Hungarians. What can they do? Then the Rumanians. What can they do? And what can the Germans do? There is no future for any of them. We are greater than they; through our culture we stand up to all of them. And you will see that they will be only too glad to follow our lead in their hopeless position."

What is this but the basest chauvinism? Could Hitler have done better? In the same vein M. Kopecky, Minister of Propaganda (and also a member of the Communist Party, whose battle-cry was once "Workers of the world, unite! ") said this at Reichenberg in the autumn of last year:

"Liberec will never again be Reichenberg. We will clear Liberec of the German enemies . . . so thoroughly that not the smallest place will remain where the German seed could grow once more. We shall expel all the Germans, we shall confiscate their property, we shall de-nationalise not only the town but the whole area . . . so that the victorious spirit of *Slavdom* [my italics] shall permeate the country from the frontier to the interior."

This is racialist lunacy in the service of hysterical nationalism. The parallel, indeed, with Hitlerism is startling. Miss Sheila Grant Duff, who is what is called in the idiotic phrase strongly "pro-Czech", wrote from Prague in *The Manchester Guardian* of October 26th 1945 as follows:

"The Sudeten Germans wear *discriminating armbands*. They

are given the rations [i.e. starvation rations] which they themselves gave *to the Jews* . . . They are removed from their homes and sent to work *like cattle*, with no hope of redress. Their property is simply confiscated, and their labour is little more than *slave labour*. *But* . . . the Czechs . . . are *not Nazis*. I have traced no one single case of organised beating ; I have heard of no acts, once the revolts were over, of deliberate cruelty or brutality."

All the italics are mine.

No one in his senses would suggest that all "the Czechs", or the majority of them, are Nazis or anything like it : but for the rest, may I ask Miss Duff how precisely she defines a Nazi? Not, apparently, as someone who brands human beings with a mark of racial shame : or who starves them : or who treats them like cattle : or who uses them as slaves. No : for the sensitive conscience of 1945 an additional characteristic is necessary before a man can qualify as a Nazi—namely "deliberate cruelty or brutality".

Well, perhaps Miss Duff will attend to the following. This is what was written by G. E. R. Gedye, whom I have already mentioned, in *The Daily Herald* of October 9th, after returning to Vienna from Czechoslovakia, where he had inspected a camp in which Sudeten Germans were confined while awaiting expulsion :

"I was able to visit one of these concentration camps. Let me say at once that it was not a Belsen.

"Nobody was actually tortured there, nobody murdered, no bodies lay around unburied.

"But I have no hesitation in qualifying it as a 'horror camp', although all the inmates agreed it was a 'good' camp compared with others they had been in.

"They were crowded together in huts regardless of age or sex . . .

"Their ages varied from four days to 80 years. Everyone looked starved . . .

"The most shocking sight was that of the babies with which most huts were filled.

"One woman sat with a medicine bottle full of mothers' milk —there is no other milk in the camp—trying to moisten the lips of something which she called her baby.

44

"Two months old, it was smaller than a healthy newborn baby. It had a wizened monkey-like face, dark brown skin stretched taut over the bones, arms like matchsticks—a starving baby.

"Near her stood another mother holding a shrunken bundle of skin and bones, smaller than a normal two-months-old baby. I stared incredulously when she told me it was 14 months old.

"In one bed a young blonde girl lay in pain, holding in her arms the infant to which she had given birth—without medical aid—24 hours previously, amid the hubbub of the surrounding crowd of men, women and children.

"On the next two bunks lay two aged women as though dead. Only close observation showed both were still faintly breathing. Like the babies, they were dying of hunger . . .

"I have no fear of being accused of sentimental tenderness for the Nazis when I describe these camps as an outrage to humanity and the good name of the Czechoslovak nation.

"Neither the Government nor the population at large can be aware of these horrors, or they would be stopped tomorrow."

Is Miss Duff still inclined to preserve her nice distinction as to what does and does not constitute a Nazi? And if so, is she of one mind, I wonder, with Masaryk—I mean the great Masaryk —who first became famous, in less indecent days, for saving from intolerant racialists the life of a single unimportant Jew?

This madness, as I have said, is not peculiar to the Czechs. It is rampant in varying degrees throughout Europe today, and unless it is halted it will end by destroying us.

*   *   *   *

The third development on the Continent of Europe is the reversion to a more barbaric concept of justice.

The typically western practice, which with Socratism and the Judaeo-Christian doctrine of personality is one of the three great pillars of our civilisation, obeys two clearly defined and generally recognised rules, which are as follows : (a) A man is in danger of punishment only if he breaks a law which was a law at the time of the alleged offence, and (b) A man may be punished only after a fair trial. This practice has no doubt been more firmly established and more generally followed in England than anywhere else in Europe, but it had for some time, until a comparatively recent date, been winning steadier and steadier acceptance over large areas of the Continent. Now the whole movement is in the opposite direction.

I shall waste no words about the concentration camps with which Europe is still honeycombed and into which men disappear, without trial and simply because they are unpalatable to the ruling group, and are sometimes never heard of again. All but a tiny minority in this country loathe the very thought of them. But there is another aspect of the matter about which there seems surprisingly little disquiet. I mean the execution or lengthy imprisonment of leaders, often after the caricature of a trial which is worse than no trial at all, simply for the offence of having been on the losing side.

Here, I know, I am on delicate ground, and unless I am careful I shall be accused of sympathy with fascism. On the contrary, it is because I detest fascism that I watch these proceedings with grave misgiving. For they mark, it seems to me, a collapse into the intolerance, the savagery, the revenge, the extra-legal exercise of power, and the dismissal of a man's motives as irrelevant, which are among the worst characteristics of fascism itself.

There was an inconspicuous line or so in some of the newspapers a few weeks ago, informing those who happened to see them that Mr. Tanner, the social democrat who had been active in the defence of Finland when she was attacked by the Soviet Union, and who had later helped to take his country into war against the latter as an ally of or co-belligerent with the Nazis, had been sentenced to five and a half years' imprisonment. I well remember the Labour Party Conference of 1940 at which Mr. D. N. Pritt's expulsion on the Finnish question was debated, and I can still hear Mr. Philip Noel-Baker's impassioned speech in defence of "our socialist comrades" in Finland. I have looked it up, and here are some extracts:

"But it seemed to us that all his [Mr. Pritt's] great efforts were directed to a single end—to defend the Government of Moscow's action in attacking Finland, which the Party have repeatedy condemned; and to attack, and, if he will forgive the word, to vilify the Government of Finland, in which many of our Socialist comrades have taken part, and which the Party has sought to encourage and support . . .

"That seemed to us a very serious thing. . . The issue of aggression is the greatest single question in world politics today, and all our hopes of Socialism depend on whether we can make an international system by which aggression shall be re-

46

strained. . . When Finland was attacked it was our duty, and we fulfilled it, to denounce the aggression. It was denounced by the National Council of Labour, the Parliamentary Party, the Trades Union Congress, and the Labour and Socialist International. But Mr. Pritt pursued a different policy of his own. He made every effort in his power, as it seemed to us, to oppose, discredit, and defeat the policy which we believe to be vital to the salvation of mankind. . .

"In Finland there is a Socialist Party; it has 85 members in the Diet out of 200; and it has had a Socialist Government, with Agrarian help, for the last four years. It is by far the strongest Party both in the Government and in the State. The Trade Union Movement is a growing power. It has a Co-operative Movement to which more than half the population of the country now belong. At that time the Foreign Minister was our comrade Tanner, a delegate to Moscow, leader of the Socialist Party, leader of the Co-operative Movement, elected to the presidency of the International Co-operative Alliance with the support of the Soviet Union, and recommended for the presidency of Finland in 1937 in a manifesto signed by the Comintern official, Otto Kuusinen himself. These men were our comrades, as good Socialists as we are, or even as Mr. Pritt. . .

"Of course, they [Finland] are a Democracy. Of course they were united—as we found by our delegation—united to a man behind their Government. Even men who had called themselves Communists had gone over openly against the Russian aggression. . ."

That, of course, was before Germany attacked the Soviet Union and Finland lined up with her. This action of Finland was unquestionably deplorable. Whatever the provocation, however natural her desire to recover the territories which Russia had —what is the word?—had taken from her, and however great her fear of becoming a Soviet satellite, alliance or co-belligerency with the Nazis ought to have been in all circumstances unthinkable. But about two things there is, if not certainty, then probability of a high degree. The first is that Mr. Tanner acted from genuinely patriotic motives not at all of an unworthy kind, and the second is that the majority of the Finnish people were with him. That he committed no offence in law is absolutely certain—for otherwise why would it have been necessary to pass *post factum*, and for the specific purpose of trying him and others, the law of September 12th 1945 for punishment of war

47

criminals, but of war criminals since 1941 only? Yet simply because his policy failed he is sentenced to a savage term of imprisonment, whereas if it had succeeded he would have been a national hero. It is pretty certain that the Finns have acted under Soviet pressure, and must therefore be excused; but that cannot modify the effect of the sentence on European political life.

General Mihailovitch is being " tried " by Marshal Tito as a war criminal or Yugoslav traitor—I am not sure, and do not much care, which. Mr. Ernest Bevin has clarified some of the facts about Mihailovitch, and what he said is confirmed and amplified from other sources. Mihailovitch is a sincere patriot of a type (very much not my type) which is quite familiar in this country. As a patriot of any sort, he detested foreign domination : as a Serb, he disliked Croat ascendancy; and as a conservative, he feared communism. He admittedly rendered great service to our cause during the second half of 1941, and indeed was the first to organise resistance against the Nazis. What happened later is in dispute, though he was thanked by General Eisenhower as late as New Year's Day of 1943. By the end of that year, says Mr. Bevin, he was no longer fighting the Germans, and some of his lieutenants were actively cooperating with them against the partisans. Others deny this, or believe that his lieutenants were acting without his authority. I prefer to believe Mr. Bevin. But, even on the worst interpretation, it seems pretty clear that he collaborated with the Nazis, if he did collaborate with them, not because he liked them or wanted them to win, but because that seemed to him the best immediate way of saving his country from Croat domination and communism. He was utterly wrong: as in the case of Tanner, any collaboration with the Nazis, whatever the motive, ought to have been the one thing which no right-minded man could possibly consider. But are miscalculation, stupidity, blimpishness, or even reactionary political tendencies a proper passport for the firing squad or gallows? For shot or hanged he will certainly be, and his trial will be a farce. The State Department sent a Note to the Jugoslav Government in which it requested that certain Americans should be given an opportunity to testify. The Note recalled that Mihailovitch had contributed materially to the allied cause : that American liaison officers were with him during most of the period of his military activity : that many American airmen were rescued and returned to the allied lines through "the undaunted efforts of the General's forces": and that a number of these rescued airmen, and others in the United States closely associated with the General and with first-hand evidence bearing on the charges of collaboration with the enemy, wished to give evidence. The request was refused, on the ground that Mihailovitch's crimes against the Jugoslav people were so great that "discussion as to guilt or otherwise could not be allowed." The Jugoslav Government thought fit to add that "full justice will be applied during the interrogation and trial of the traitor Draza Mihailovitch". Full justice when you assume a man's guilt and rule out effective, spoken evidence for the defence! I know that permission to send written evidence has been conceded; but in the conditions of a trial like this written evidence means little or nothing.

Almost every day there is news of someone else, some soldier or politician, who has been hanged or shot or guillotined or imprisoned perhaps for life. What is going to be the effect of all this on European politics? If the ins feel quite certain that they'll be killed when they're out, won't they cling to power by every possible device of brutality and suppression? Won't decent men avoid politics like the plague? Isn't there a danger that the whole scene will degenerate into one of intolerance, illegalism and savagery?

The reply will be that quislings and traitors must be prevented from doing further mischief. Certainly: but beware lest, in the process, you help to establish in another form the things for which you condemn them, and cannot condemn them too strongly. The worst of these men—the crudely ambitious and the fascist-minded, not the blimps or the muddle-heads or, like Tanner, the sincerely misguided—wanted Hitler to win: they approved of his savage philosophy, or at any rate were prepared to accept it as the price of their own aggrandizement. Beware, I say, lest you give them and Hitler a posthumous victory.

Apart from a basic objection to the death penalty in any circumstances, for I regard it as a blasphemous obscenity, decent ways could be found of rendering genuinely dangerous people harmless if the will were there. Pétain, in spite of his age, was in some ways, as a symbolic figure, more dangerous than Laval; but they killed Laval, because public opinion permitted or demanded it, and put Pétain in quite safe and humanly tolerable confinement because it didn't. It is absurd to pretend that Tanner, even if left completely at large, would have been in any genuine sense dangerous at all. What could he have done, with the Finnish Government under the strict surveillance of the Soviet Union? He might, it may be said, have gradually organised some sort of movement for the recovery of Finnish territories. If he could indeed have done so by democratic means, preventing him would seem hardly democratic: if he had attempted antidemocratic means, he could have been stopped immediately. The probability is that, decently and honourably treated, he would have worked in the new situation for the success of Finish-Soviet relations, just as Smuts became a lifelong friend of Britain after the liberal settlement of the Boer war. As it is, they have made a martyr of him: and a martyr always has followers, at large but underground, who are biding their time.

Let us be honest, and confess that a good number of these savage sentences are nothing but naked revenge.

※   ※   ※   ※

The transition to the Nuremberg trials, which are an Allied rather than a European affair, requires no feat of literary construction. There is something to be said in favour of them, and they are being conducted, in so far as such trials ever could be conducted, very fairly indeed. At one time I thought that the arguments in their favour might possibly just balance, or even outweigh, the arguments against. But the pleas with which they have been defended by King's Counsel and other eminent persons in the columns of *The Times* have made me revise this opinion.

The objections can be put down under three heads, though in fact each objection largely implies the others. They are, first, that the conquerors, and only the conquerors, are trying the conquered: secondly, that even while we try them we are ourselves doing some of the very things for which we try them; and thirdly that entering into a conspiracy to wage aggressive war, which is the crux of the whole matter, is not a crime at all.

1. *The conquerors are trying the conquered.* "So we believe" said Sir Hartley Shawcross in his speech of December 4th 1945 "that this Tribunal, acting, as we know it will act notwithstanding its appointment, in a world in which hardly any neutrals were left, by the victorious powers, with complete and judicial objectivity, will provide a contemporary touchstone. . . ." The implied apology seems a lame one. The

neutrals include Sweden and Switzerland, two of the most civilised peoples in the modern world; and the representation of even one of them among the judges would have made Sir Hartley's "complete" a little more reasonable and his "notwithstanding" a little less necessary.* Again "Let the defendants and their protagonists" said Sir Hartley in the same speech "complain that the Charter is in this as in other matters an *ex parte* fiat of the victor. These victors, composing as they do the overwhelming majority of the nations of the world, represent also the world's sense of justice. . . ." Sir Hartley is surely committing—perforce—precisely the error that was uncovered in our discussion of liberty of speech. He is convinced that on this issue the victors represent the world's sense of justice : so are nine hundred and ninety nine out of a thousand in every victor country : so, by and large, am I. But the principles of western law surely rest on a realisation that no one can be a judge in his own cause : and that even if ten million are of one opinion and half a dozen of another, the ten million may not judge the half-dozen in a dispute between them.

There is another objection no less fundamental. The avowed object of the trials, and their justification, is to punish crimes committed by nations against humanity as a whole : but this object is at once made suspect by the fact that it is nations, and not men, that are sitting in judgment. Are there no representatives of humanity among the neutrals of Europe or elsewhere? Or among the Jews, who have suffered so cruelly? Or among the Austrians, or the Italians, or the Germans themselves? Only if they too were sitting on the daïs at Nuremberg could history record that this indeed was a Tribunal of mankind.

2. *We are doing some of the things for which we try them.* I pass hurriedly over our bombing, while the trial was actually in progress, of an open Indonesian village, explicitly by way of reprisal ("Early today Pübadak was wiped out by the R.A.F.") : for this was a triviality, though a very shameful one, in comparison with Lidice and Oradour-sur-Glane and Saint

---

* It is highly significant that the words "in a world in which hardly any neutrals were left," while included in the text of the speech as circulated to the Press on December 3rd, were apparently not actually spoken, for an erratum note deleting them was issued on the same day. Presumably it was felt that these words made the contradiction inherent in the whole sentence, and sufficiently indicated by the word "notwithstanding," needlessly explicit.

Dié and the rest. But there are other actions not so easy to dismiss by the argument of even comparative innocence.

One of the crimes for which these men are being tried is "deportation and other inhumane acts committed against any civilian population." But before the summer is out their judges will have ordered, instigated or acquiesced in the expulsion of some fourteen million persons, with what ruthlessness I will leave the reader, when he has read a later section, to judge: and these expulsions were and are being committed at a time when military necessities could no longer be pleaded, however dishonestly, in mitigation.

A second count in the indictment is "wanton destruction of cities, towns or villages, or devastation not justified by military necessity." But while the indictment was being prepared we were exterminating, with the final devilry of atom bombs, the civilian population of two Japanese cities, without warning, without discrimination, and without the possibility of pleading that otherwise the war might have been lost. We shortened the war by a few months or a few weeks? We saved our soldiers' lives? Possibly: but that is what the Nazis plead.

I shall take the opportunity of saying a word about this business of Hiroshima and Nagasaki. *The Manchester Guardian,* one of the most consistently sane of all British papers, wrote at the time that "the use of the atom bomb against the Japanese is entirely legitimate. It is illogical to judge the morality of bombing by the size of the bomb used." This great journal was surely showing less than its usual insight. The words were correct enough, but not the implication: the statement was true to the letter, but false to the spirit.

In the devilish business of war, there is only one aim on either side, and that is to win. If therefore in a just, defensive war your best or quickest chance of winning were to submit to agonising torture all the children of the enemy, such a method of warfare would no doubt be as "logical" as the bows of Agincourt. But would it be decent, or wise, or, to use a word now almost out of currency, right? No: poised on the brink of that unspeakable wickedness, men, or all but the basest of them, would realise that they had come to a point at which formal logic was no longer valid, but must give way to spiritual reality. "Caught up as we are in the historical process" they would say "we are compelled to do vile things, lest even viler should befall. We have no alternative but to bomb and burn the enemy. But the deliberate mass torturing of children is a vileness not merely new in degree, but new and worse in kind. For the sake of the whole span of time and the whole brotherhood of men, we dare not submit the human currency to this further debasement, which would be followed by another, and still another, on to a fearful end that no one can foresee. Logic may say 'you shall': but some instinct higher and deeper than logic, some sense of a trusteeship which we can only dimly comprehend, says imperatively 'You shall not.'"

I say that by using the atom bomb we committed just this further debasement of the human currency. Apply so much heat to water, and it is still water: apply a little more, and it is steam. What was up to a point a quantitative change has become, as the Marxists say, a qualitative one. And so in the present case. The atom bomb was not merely two thousand times more powerful than the biggest and best of the previous bombs: by very reason of that power it was something new in kind—a threat, and for the first time, to the very existence of humanity. By our blasphemous presumption in using it we took another step to the abyss: by renouncing its use we might have staggered back to moral sanity.

To return, however, to Nuremberg. A third charge relates to the breach of international obligations. But only a week or so before this writing Russia, one of Germany's judges, committed a breach of her international obligations to Persia. She may have had good reason for doing so, but that is not the point: the breach was committed. One of the most revealing episodes in the whole course of the trials was when Herr Goering's Counsel asked to put in a document embodying accusations published as a German State Paper in 1941. Rejecting the document as irrelevant, Lord Justice Lawrence commented: "We are here to judge major war criminals, not to try the Prosecuting Powers."

Our enemies are also indicted for having broken the Geneva Convention. But we—the Allies—are breaking it wholesale, not in the letter but in the spirit, at this very moment. I am anxious to avoid easy talk about "slave labour": let it only be said, then, that nearly a year after the end of the war many millions of German prisoners are being kept at work in foreign countries, or being bandied from one country to another, and are told nothing, and can hope nothing, about the date of their release. "When belligerents call for an Armistice Convention" says Article 75 of the Convention "they shall normally cause to be

53

included therein provisions concerning the repatriation of Prisoners of War. If it has not been possible to insert in that Convention such stipulations, the belligerents shall, nevertheless, enter into communication with each other on the question as soon as possible." I shall be told, of course, that there was unconditional surrender, which is not an armistice; yes, but that, as Mr. Churchill has made quite clear, puts an even greater obligation on "civilised and Christian nations."

I wish this were all. The Government states that "since the German surrender it has not been possible to carry out the Geneva Conventions in all respects owing to situations having arisen which were never contemplated when they were drawn up, but His Majesty's Government continue to observe the spirit of the Conventions. There has been no Protecting Power since 14th May, 1945, when the Swiss Government themselves withdrew from representing German interests." Is this a just statement of the position? Are we really acting as any Protecting Power would have required? I cannot think so. I say nothing about allegations in a responsible newspaper and in the House that some of our prisoners have been underfed, for these are being officially investigated as I write; nor about France, where conditions have frequently been scandalous; nor about Russia (not a signatory to the Convention) about which in this matter we know very little. But it is certainly the fact that our prisoners get from sixpence to a shilling a day, on jobs for which the trade union rate might be say twelve or twenty-four times that amount: the argument apparently being that their Government (which doesn't exist) should be crediting them with their full soldiers' pay and should hand over the accumulation on their return. Finally, they were not enabled until recently to communicate with their relatives: and we can appreciate in a dim sort of way what this must mean when we remember that many of these prisoners are husbands of those miserable women who have been expelled from their homes in the East, and, wandering wretchedly with their children, have had nowhere to turn for help or even sympathy.

* * * *

My insistence that we have done and are doing some of the things for which we sit in judgment on our enemies must not be taken to imply that in my opinion the account is nicely balanced. On the contrary, when I read the fifty pages of the Nuremberg Indictment I can still hardly believe that such infamy could have been possible. But I also find it disagreeable to reflect that to a *tu quoque* from the enemy the reply would be a little less crushing than might be desired.

3. *Aggressive war, and conspiracies to wage it, are not crimes.* They have indeed been the rule almost since the birth of civilisation. Old-fashioned histories of Europe, to mention one continent only, devote nearly all their space to the record of one aggressive war after another. Louis the Fourteenth, Peter the Great, Frederick the Great, Catherine, Joseph the Second, Gustavus the Fourth, Napoleon, Napoleon the Third, Nicholas the First, Bismarck—these are the names of some aggressors in the couple of centuries between the Congress of Westphalia in 1648 and the Danish War of 1864. The ambition of the Nazis was vaster—or vaster than anyone's since Napoleon : their methods were far viler—though the vulgar little Corsican massacred all his prisoners at Jaffa : their victory would have been followed, indeed their defeat has been followed, by horrors worse than anything since the Thirty Years' War. But as we read the story of man's secular wickedness, as we shudder at the engravings of Callot and Goya, do we not conclude that Hitler was doing, with more ferocity and with twentieth-century technique, what men of many nations had done before him when they thought they had the power to satisfy their ambitions?

There is no law, I repeat—no law properly so called—against either aggressive war or a conspiracy to wage it, and that is the essential point. The Kellogg Pact is cited to prove the contrary : and it is on this that Sir Hartley Shawcross, with a great deal of special pleading, has in the main relied. The Pact, it is said, outlawed war ; and the Germans were a party to it. But if we are trying to find the truth, and not to debate with one another, must we not confess that every international engagement of the kind, every bilateral or multilateral treaty, has always been entered into with a whole armoury of mental reservations, and above all with the proviso *rebus sic stantibus?* It is shocking that it should be so, but so it has always been. We went so far, in fact, as to make our own reservations to the Kellogg Pact explicit. '' The language of Article 1, as to the renunciation of war as an instrument of national policy '' wrote Sir Austen Chamberlain to the United States Ambassador on May 19th 1928 '' renders it desirable that I should remind your Excellency that there are certain regions of the world the welfare and integrity of which constitute a special and vital interest for our peace and safety. His Majesty's Government have been at pains to make it clear in the past that inter-ference with these regions cannot be suffered. Their protection against attack is to the British Empire a measure of self-defence. It must be clearly understood that His Majesty's Government in Great Britain accept the new Treaty upon the distinct under-standing that it does not prejudice their freedom of action in this respect. The Government of the United States have comparable interests, any disregard of which by a foreign Power they have declared that they would regard as an unfriendly act. His Majesty's Government believe, therefore, that in defining their position they are expressing the intention and meaning of the United States Government." "Certain [unspecified] regions of the world." "A special and vital interest." If you examine the whole statement carefully, you will see that it could be used to justify any possible breach of the Kellogg Pact.

And if our own reservations were the most sweeping, those of others were substantial enough. The United States Government excepted from the operation of the Pact any action for the main-tenance of the Monroe Doctrine—which was what she really cared about ; and France specifically reserved any war of self-defence or in fulfilment of treaty obligations—it being well known that while many wars really are in self-defence, as ours was in 1939, every war of aggression can be, and is, dressed up as a war of self-defence, or for special and vital interests, or whatever it may be. In fact, and not to be too nice about it, the Kellogg Pact was one of the greatest pieces of bunkum in the whole sorry history of international pacification. This became apparent when Japan, one of the signatories to the Pact, invaded Man-churia in 1931. What did we do about it? Literally rather less than nothing. Mr. Amery's speech, quoted so often, is worth quoting again in this connection. "I confess" he said on February 27th 1933 "that I see no reason why, either in act or in word or in sympathy, we should go individually or internation-ally against Japan in this matter. . . . Our whole policy in India, our whole policy in Egypt, stand condemned if we condemn Japan. . . . I am afraid there is a good deal of conscious or unconscious hypocrisy when we talk about the League of Nations, about disarmament and about peace. . . . At any rate, I have freed my soul this afternoon." The attitude of men like Mr. Amery was disastrous, for it was of the unchecked aggression in 1931 that 1939 was the ghastly sequel : but he was being honest, and was by no means speaking for himself alone.

At this very moment, Kellogg Pact or no Kellogg Pact, Uno or no Uno, is not the possibility of war from some quarter or another the major assumption that guides the policy of every great and medium Power in the world? National sovereignty, of course, is the root of the trouble : the conception that every country is its own master when it really comes to the point—when its "vital interests," that is to say, are concerned. Is there the slightest sign that the most powerful nations in the modern world are moving away from that conception? In spite of genuine desires, I believe, in this and other countries, the movement is, on the contrary, all the other way. The United Nations, with their Veto—for that is the essential point—are farther away from any genuine modification of national sovereignty than was the Wilson-inspired internationalism of 1919.

National life in a civilised community is conducted on the presumption that the law against theft and rape and murder will, by and large, be obeyed ; international life is conducted on the presumption that war is always to be feared, because no law against it, genuinely accepted and with the necessary sanctions, so much as exists.

But what we are doing at Nuremberg, it is said alternatively, is precisely to create this law, and simultaneously to provide it with sanctions. I know, I know : that is the overwhelming argument in favour of these trials, and the utmost weight should be given to it. My misgivings, nevertheless, remain. It might be pointed out that one of the countries creating this law was herself an accomplice in what it is now sought to establish as a crime : for by the Nazi-Soviet Pact Russia became, in fact if not in name, a co-belligerent with Hitler in the rape of Poland —worse, she "entered into a conspiracy" with him to carve that country up, and proceeded to do so. And the rape of Poland, as Sir Hartley insists, was itself the unleashing of the war for which the Nazis had previously conspired. Further, three pages of the Indictment are devoted to "The Acquiring of Totalitarian Control of Germany : Political" for the purpose of entering into the conspiracy. Parts of them can be read, with the change of hardly a word, as a description of "the acquiring of totalitarian control" in the Soviet Union—though the aim in that case, of course, was not aggressive war. But the real objection is more fundamental. The very essence of western justice is that a man is in danger of punishment only if he breaks a law which was a law at the time of the alleged offence. That is a principle which, in the world as it is today, must above all be strengthened, not weakened. How do you strengthen it by means of *post factum* legislation—for that is what it really is, in spite of all Sir Hartley Shawcross's rather uneasy denials? How can you establish law by acting, on the strict interpretation, illegally?

As I see it, there is confusion at Nuremberg between sins and crimes. These men have committed sins unspeakable; but subject to correction from those who really understand these matters, I would say that many of the offences with which they are charged can be described as crimes only " by way of the corruption of language " of which the Attorney-General complains. It is certainly essential that they should be prevented from doing further mischief: and those who believe in retributive punishment will rightly hold that they should suffer it, though the same should then apply in varying degree to men of other countries, and not to quislings only. For my own part, though I shall no doubt be thought crazy for saying so, I should prefer the technique not of punishment but of cure. However that may be, would it not have been better if, instead of being tried by their victors on the basis of law, they had been arraigned for their sins by an international body (including a number of their own countrymen) representing the conscience of civilised mankind? And would it not have been better if, meanwhile, we had refrained from sin ourselves? My fear now is that, when temporary passions have passed and history has her say, these trials may be seen, in Germany and elsewhere, not as a new start and the first firm establishment of international justice, but as a further exercise of arbitrary power, a sanctification, not of law, but of " woe to the vanquished."

IV

I come at length to the subject of communism,

It used to be fashionable, and is becoming fashionable again, to say that there is little to choose between communism and fascism. In some respects this is true ; and it is important to consider just how far it is true and how far it is false.

The values which moved the founders of Marxian communism —the values which were their end, the values they wished to establish in the society they hoped to build—were not the fascist values : they were the values of western civilisation, with respect for personality at the heart of them. The free development of personality, they thought and rightly thought, was impossible for average men and women so long as they lived in squalor and insecurity and want: and it was impossible, also, until self-government were to become a matter, not of the ballot-box only, but of daily and especially of economic life as well. Hitler wished to destroy our values : Karl Marx to establish them more securely, and to give them a wider application and a deeper meaning. For Hitler the Rights of Man were anathema : they were Marx's gospel. The State, said Marx, must wither away : no, said Hitler, it must exercise an unchanging tyranny not merely for a thousand years but for ever. The ideal society, I have suggested, is one of fully developed personalities, freely cooperating. Marx would have agreed with this statement : Hitler would have called it liberal or Marxist filth.

What, then, has gone wrong? Why is Marxian communism, which set out to realise our values more truly and fully than they had ever been realised before—why is it now, after the defeat of Hitler, the most powerful of all the forces positively establishing values that are in direct contradiction to ours? Why wherever there is Soviet power or Soviet influence is respect for personality so gravely violated? Why, instead of an ever increasing tendency towards treating *all* men—*all* men, irrespective of what they are or think or do—as being "in their own right" (for that, it must be insisted, is what respect for personality means), is the movement, under the impact of Soviet communism, all in the other direction?

The answer is that in the human interplay it is means and not ends that are the effective reality. My end is dynamic in relation to me, in the sense that it moves me to adopt certain means ; but it is only the means that are dynamic in relation to my neighbour. Only what I actually think or do in the immediate relation can affect the other party to the relation. It is my behaviour that is socially decisive, not the reason for my behaviour. If one man kills another you show yourself civilised by considering the motive at his trial; but, whatever his motive, the second man is dead.

The aim of Marxian communism was a society in which every individual was to be physically and spiritually free. The means were rapidly to become something very different, namely the physical and spiritual enslavement of millions. How was this possible?

They looked about them, these men, and saw a world disfigured by poverty, unemployment, greed, aggression and war. They wished to substitute for it a society of free and equal men and women, secure and peaceable, satisfied materially, and each giving according to his ability and receiving according to his need. That was the vision of a communist society; and it is still, and now more than ever, the society of our dreams. But how, they asked, were they to bring it into being?

They found the root of the trouble in the system of competitive capitalism: and they were wrong only to this extent, that the system was not the ultimate but, in the modern world, the main contributory cause. Competitive capitalism, then, they said, must be overthrown, and replaced by the cooperative commonwealth. In such a country as Britain parliamentary action might conceivably suffice: but in countries where parliaments were weak or non-existent, where democracy was at best partial or ineffective, a very different method could alone produce the desired result. The dispossessed, the proletariat, the masses of the working people must seize power, exercise a dictatorship, and build a new order of cooperation, equality, justice and peace. As the young society developed, the need for dictatorship would gradually disappear; the state would wither away, and the end would be universal freedom.

This was the early programme. But already a quarter of a century ago Rosa Luxemburg noted a modification, and warned the world of its probable consequences. Effective power was seized, in the November days, not by the proletariat nor yet by what was called the class-conscious vanguard of the proletariat: it was seized by a small group of men, an élite, which took it upon itself to interpret the interests of the proletariat. Already side by side or within the dictatorship of the proletariat there were the beginnings of a dictatorship over the proletariat.

There was another grave danger, this time in the thought of Marx himself. History was made, he insisted, primarily by the interplay of economic relations. It is quite untrue that he gave no weight to other factors : he gave, on the contrary, a very great deal to the influence of ideas, and of everything that is called "the superstructure", once they had acquired, after their birth from economic relations, a life and validity of their own. On the other hand, there is such a passion in his stressing of economic relations that everything else is dim by comparison ; and I have no doubt that his insistence on materialism in the technical sense, an insistence prompted by a passion to liberate personality, has been a potent factor in the spread of materialism in the popular sense, and in the growth of contempt for the very personality that Marx desired to liberate. On the other side of the account, and by way of comment on Marx's theory, it may be noted that many rank and file communists will devote themselves in utter selflessness, and even give life itself, for the furtherance of ends from which they neither hope nor desire to obtain any material or personal benefit whatsoever.

But to return. Both dictatorships—the dictatorships of and over the proletariat—proceeded, with varying speeds at various times, to consolidate themselves. And because the end—the perfect society, the Paradise on earth—was so infinitely precious, because the happiness not only of Russia but of the whole world depended on safeguarding the foundations already laid, any method whatsoever that might contribute to the absolute power, first of both dictatorships and then, by a natural process, of the only dictatorship that mattered, the dictatorship of the ruling group, was not merely justifiable, but imperatively demanded as a matter of duty, of conscience, and of religion.

So came, where communism was in power, the political prisons, the secret police, the concentration camps, the forced labour, and the expulsion, confinement and execution of deviators and dissentients : the enforcement of a strict Party line— "truth is what the Party thinks" : an absolute censorship : and the attempt to mould even men's minds to uniformity by all the arts of suggestion and propaganda. So came, too, where communism was not in power, the political, social and psychological characteristics that are so familiar. Just as communists inside Russia must safeguard the foundations of the new society by any means, so must communists outside Russia, also by any means, serve the interests of the Soviet power in every immediate situation. But they must do more than that: they must make the Soviet Union finally secure, and must at the same time build communism in their own countries, by increasing their strength and influence, again by any means, as rapidly as possible. If this could be done most effectively by the suppression of the true and the suggestion of the false: by taking as their criterion not the facts of any matter but how that matter might "best" be "put": by concealing their real intentions behind façades: by discrediting opponents simply for the sake of discrediting them, the accuracy or otherwise of what they might think it desirable to allege being completely irrelevant: and by such clever manoeuvring as would give them, in however small a minority they might be, a control more or less absolute over organisations that could serve their purpose—then methods like these were not merely permissible, they were obligatory. And something else was obligatory too. They must school their own hearts and their own minds to a rigid, an automatic, an unquestioning obedience to the Party line. Once that line had been laid down they must do more than act, they must think, in accordance with it. The possibility that it might be wrong must simply not occur to them. And if nevertheless some such dangerous thought did occur, they must have so conditioned themselves that they would at once find good reasons for expelling it from their minds.

This is the communist practice and the communist mentality both inside and outside Russia today. It is an antiliberal, antiwestern, antichristian practice and mentality: its characteristic is not respect for personality—the treating of all men, of all men indifferently, including ourselves, as "being in their own right"—but the precise opposite: namely the treating of men, including ourselves, not as ends in themselves but as means to an outside end. And it is necessary to repeat, what is the crucial point, that this practice and this mentality are dictated by considerations of duty and conscience, and that the communist does and is what he does and is as a matter of religion.

I do not for a moment mean that the communist religion is a religion of evil in the sense that the Nazi religion is a religion of evil. The communist does not think of power and ruthlessness and expediency as good in and for themselves: and that is just what the Nazi does think. For Nazism, western values are,

I repeat, evil; for communism they are, for the time being at least, irrelevant. The fact is simply that, among communists, the Messianism inspired by the end has become incarnate in the method, and the method is ruthless expediency. Bourgeois morality must be religiously disregarded in so far as it impedes the coming of a higher morality. What these communists fail to understand is that history is a continuing process: that you can't advance by throwing away what you have achieved already: that the Rights of Man are the precious foundation for an even finer structure: and that if you mistreat the seed of bourgeois morality you will get no flower at all, but nihilism.

Communist morality could hardly be summed up better than in the words of Dr. Georg Lukacz, People's Commissar for Education during the Bela Kun dictatorship. A writer in *Unser Weg* of March 1921 said of him the following: "A representative theoretician, who was perhaps the sole brain behind Hungarian communism, . . . answered my question, as to whether lying and cheating of the members of the Party by their own leaders were admissible, by this statement: Communist ethics make it the highest duty to accept the necessity of acting wickedly. This, he said, was the greatest sacrifice which revolution asked from us."[*] I doubt whether any educated communist would deny in his heart that this is a true statement of the position. It is precisely the sacrificial element in communism that gives it so great an appeal to noble hearts and minds, particularly at the present time, when so many faiths are dead or dying. But the nobility does not always survive.

It ought to be unnecessary to give examples of communist morality in this country. I gave, in a previous volume[†], many hundreds of pages of them. But because the public memory is so short, I append just four quotations:

September 1939 (before the anti-war "line"): "The Communist Party supports the war, believing it to be a just war, which should be supported by the whole working class and all friends of democracy in Britain." (Harry Pollitt in *How to Win the War*)

---

[*] F. Borkenau, *The Communist International*, Faber & Faber, 1938.

[†] *The Betrayal of the Left*, Gollancz, 1941.

October 1939 (after the anti-war "line"): "We are against the continuance of the war. We demand that negotiations be immediately opened for the establishment of peace in Europe." (*Daily Worker*, October 4th 1939)

November 1939: "This is an Imperialist war, like the war of 1914. It is a sordid exploiters' war of rival millionaire groups, using the workers as their pawns in their struggle for world domination, for markets, colonies and profits, for the oppression of peoples. This is a war to which no worker in any country can give support." (Mr. R. Palme Dutt, one of the leading communist theoreticians, in *Why This War?*, published by the Communist Party in November 1939)

February 1940: "Against this historical fact there is no reply. Britain declared war, not Germany. Attempts were made to end the war, but the Soviet-German peace efforts were rejected by Britain. All through these months the British and French Governments have had the power to end the war. They have chosen to extend it. . . . War should never have been declared on September 3rd." (*Daily Worker*, February 1st 1940)

Everyone remembers that immediately Germany invaded Russia the communists again became enthusiastically pro-war, so no quotations for that period are necessary. So enthusiastic were they, indeed, that you might have wondered, as you watched them hunting down "semi-fascism" in all sorts of unlikely places, whether all the rest of us weren't crypto-defeatists. But perhaps, you will say, there was something honest, in the ordinary meaning of the word, about all this? Perhaps there really was a sense in which the war was antifascist in September 1939, Imperialist in October 1939 and antifascist again in the autumn of 1941? Well, British communists prefer to be silent about that: but Stalin is less discreet. "The second World War against the Axis States" he said a few months ago "assumed *from the very beginning* the character of an antifascist war of liberation, and one of its tasks was the restoration of democratic freedoms." It would never have occurred to him to explain why, if this was so, he said in reply to birthday greetings from Hitler and Ribbentrop on December 27th 1939 "the friendship of the peoples of Germany and the Soviet Union, cemented by blood, has every reason to be lasting and firm." The blood in question was that jointly spilled in the rape of Poland.

The fact of course is that truth just didn't come into the matter at all. Soviet tactics demanded that an antifascist war should be called an Imperialist war: this was a lie: it was a matter of religion to support Soviet tactics: it was a matter of religion, therefore, to lie. The real tragedy is that after a day or two the lying wasn't even conscious.

I don't know whether any of my non-communist readers have ever tried to argue with communists about the Soviet Union, or the Party "line," or indeed any aspect of national or international politics. The thing just can't be done. One can argue with a Tory, even if he is much stupider and more prejudiced than one is oneself, as is occasionally the case: for however violently he may be defending his party and attacking yours— and you, of course, are doing the same the other way about— your basic assumptions are the same, unless of course he's a downright fascist. Both assume that the object of a discussion is, in theory at least, to discover the truth: both may disregard the theory, but that's another matter. But in a discussion between a communist and a non-communist, the communist assumes nothing whatever of the kind. You, the non-communist, are engaged, perhaps feebly and with a considerable admixture of dishonesty, in what you think is a joint investigation: he, often very brilliantly, is "putting it across." Sometimes, particularly in raw recruits and just after a change in the "line," there is self-conscious falsification: far more often the automatism of the process precludes any consciousness that truth is being traversed—or rather ignored, for truth as well as falsehood may be useful for achieving the mate. So there is an iron curtain between the disputants: their minds never meet. Does it sound ignoble, this communist procedure? If so, the impression is false: for their loyalty is not to the truth but to something which they think or feel to be higher. And their loyalty to it is usually far more wholehearted than yours to truth: indeed, it is absolute.

This specialised idealism is to be found in every aspect of communist behaviour. In times of peace, an ordinary spy spies for money, or excitement, or at best (if he's spying for his own country) from patriotic motives of a queerly narrow kind; but a British or French or Australian communist who gives some national secret to the Soviet Union is obeying what he considers a larger patriotism, for he is helping the communist fatherland.

and so ultimately the world. A communist spy is particularly dangerous—on normal considerations of national security—not because he's a scoundrel but because he isn't.

*   *   *   *

It is the utter opposition between the western and the communist religions that so many writers overlook. The *Times* newspaper, for instance, commented as follows on Mr. Churchill's Fulton speech:

" Indeed, a clearer recognition of two points might well serve to mitigate on both sides some of the asperities of recent exchanges. The first is that there are many forms of government intermediate between western democracy and Communism, and some of them may be better adapted at the present stage of development to the requirements of Eastern Europe or of the Middle or Far East. The second is that, while western democracy and Communism are in many respects opposed, they have much to learn from each other—Communism in the working of political institutions and in the establishment of individual rights, western democracy in the development of economic and social planning."

That is in many ways excellently said; but it misses, or at any rate slurs over, an essential point. The fact is not merely that " western democracy and communism are in many respects opposed ": the fact is rather that in the most vital respect of all they are totally opposed. The religion of the West—I use the word religion in the broadest possible sense—is, as we have seen, based on treating men as being in their own right : and the whole direction had been until quite recently towards a greater and greater acceptance, both in theory and in practice, of this way of life and thought. So far as means are concerned—and means alone are effective in their impact on the world—the religion of communism is based on the exact opposite—on treating men as instruments. Moreover, this religion is a very fanatical and proselytising religion. Finally, just as in the West the general direction has been towards an increasing acceptance of respect for personality, so in communist thought and practice the tendency to treat men as instruments has been steadily becoming, in spite of some ups and downs, more and more nearly absolute.

Between these two religions there can be, in the nature of the

66

case, no compromise. They are essentially contradictory: there is no meeting-place, no half-way house, between them. To weaken by a jot or for an instant in our determination to safeguard our values would be, quite literally, to betray civilisation; and I have no doubt that the communists, on their side, think the same. Well, then, there is nothing for it but to stand firm and fight it out; by which I am not thinking, God forbid, of atom bombs, but of steadfastness in act, of frankness in speech, and above everything of an utter devotion in thought and practice to our own ideals, and a heroic effort to spread them, by force of example, throughout the world: always with the maximum of friendliness and the minimum of strife. We shall see which side will win. We cannot know; but what I do know is that if we lose, and lose we very well may, our struggle will have an eternal reality as something good in the world's history.

The *Times* article seems to me typical of a great deal of confused thinking about the affairs of eastern Europe. It may or may not be true—it probably is—that some of these countries are not " ripe " for democracy as we know it, and that they are better adapted to "intermediate" forms of government, whatever precisely that may mean. Only those with far greater knowledge than I could be bold enough to pronounce a judgment. But that is not the real question: the real question is whether by and large, whatever the details of their organisation, and in so far as they are able, these systems serve and are designed to serve respect for personality, or serve and are designed to serve the opposite.

* * * *

It is difficult to doubt that the spread in Europe today of communist practice and communist mentality is the major force opposing, in effect if not in intention, the maintenance and fuller development of our western values. The following article, written by the Berlin correspondent of *The Manchester Guardian* on February 25th and referring to the communist agitation for an immediate fusion of the two left-wing parties, may be read by way of comment on, and illustration of, everything I have so far written:

" The leaders as well as humble members of the Social Democratic party in the Russian zone have been subject to external pressure to support the demands of the Communists. . . .

"The pressure has been exerted by means of intimidation, by the removal of people from their own districts to others, and by arrests. The circumstances surrounding the arrests have been similar to the methods employed by the Gestapo. People simply disappear. The accused are given no reason, their relatives no news of their whereabouts. This applies equally to prominent members and to smaller officials. The Communists are, in nearly all places, in possession of membership-lists of the local groups and are thus able to check the attitude of almost every individual.

"Of the more prominent members who have spoken against union on the present terms, Mr. Bryll, of the Thuringian executive, has been arrested; Mrs. Lisa Peter, wife of Magdeburg's former bürgermeister Kors Peter, who had to leave for Westphalia, has been taken into custody in Magdeburg. In Berlin Gustav Dahrendorf, who opposed fusion at the Trades Union Congress earlier this month, hurriedly left by 'plane on Thursday for the British zone. Karl Gerner, another member of the executive committee and a trade union official, has been removed from his union post.

"Documents and facts are now in Allied hands and will when released give detailed evidence of charges against the methods employed by the Communists. Virtually, though not officially, the Communists are in complete control not only of the Russian zone but also of Berlin. The present position in the former capital, which is supposed to be administrated by a 'kommandantur' composed of the four occupying Powers, amounts almost to the abnegation of Allied rule and supervision.

"The German administration of Berlin is mainly in the hands of Communists. Dr. Karl Werner, the 80-year-old Oberbürgermeister, is a mere figure-head. His first in command, Karl Maron, is a well-known Communist, and other administrative key posts, such as the departments of labour and education, are held by two Communists, Hans Jendretzky and Otto Winzer respectively, the former one of the shrewdest and most determined of politicians today. The police force is for the most part under Communist influence.

"The methods employed by the Berlin administration are based on the totalitarian principle. Arrests are made without warrant. Three judges in the American sector and one in the British sector of Berlin were recently removed from their homes and have not since been heard of. They are supposed to have pronounced sentences which were not approved by the Communists.

"The concentration camps in Sachsenhausen, near Berlin, and Buchenwald have been opened again by the Russians for political offenders. In Buchenwald, in addition, former Nazi party members are taken for six-monthly 'Schulungs-kurse' (training courses) and subsequently allowed to join the Communist party.

"The Russian-licensed press (eight daily papers as against one British, one French, and one American daily) are severely censored and are not allowed to print any comment unfavourable to the proposed 'unity front.' The message of the British Labour party to the Social Democrats was suppressed in the papers except in the British and American press, and so was Maurice Thorez's speech in France demanding the Ruhr for France. The British and American papers are forbidden in the Russian zone but are traded there illegally and fetch as much as twelve marks. Active interference with the press is also taking place. In Rostock the Social Democratic organ was compelled to print an article denouncing the promoters of a mass meeting which had passed a resolution that only a Reichsparteitag should decide the question of fusion. The origin of the article was not allowed to be disclosed.

"The general tone of the Communist-controlled newspapers and the Berlin radio is hardly distinguishable from Goebbels' propaganda. . . ."

Just as Dr. Lukacz's statement throws the clearest light on communist methods in theory, so does this *Manchester Guardian* article demonstrate them, beyond any possibility of denial, in practice.

*   *   *   *

An objection may be raised in this matter of means and ends. "I agree" it might be said "that it is means and not ends that are effective in their impact on, in their transformation of, society. I agree that what you have called our western values are supremely precious, and that communist means appear to be endangering them. But for all that, and in the final interest of those values themselves, may not the communist position be right? Competitive capitalism menaces the world with poverty and war: and poverty and war must destroy those values. The decisive break came when Russia abolished competitive capitalism, and laid at least the foundations of a cooperative society. The methods then and since employed have at any rate preserved those foundations, so far as a sixth of the world's surface is concerned: competitive capitalism has not reappeared there. When the position is finally secure, may there not be a reversal of the present direction? May not respect for personality come into its own, and in a finer and more complete form than we have ever known? After all, the Russian Revolution is only a quarter of a century old."

I sympathise with this objection, for I have shared it. Any time between 1919 and 1933 I hated—only my own heart can know how much I hated— the growing ruthlessness of the Soviet régime. I not only hated it, I thought it both unnecessary and dangerous. But the fact that over that great area competitive capitalism had been abolished was something to gladden the heart, and to give what support one could to the young society seemed an obvious duty. Year after year I thought "The end, the full flowering of our western values, remains: the means will change: the State will begin to wither away." From 1933 to 1939 the ruthlessness increased, and so did my hatred of it: but support seemed more than ever imperative, for Russia was the strongest bulwark against the arch-enemy of the West, Hitler's fascism. It was the shock of the Nazi-Soviet Pact—merely, I think, because this was a supreme instance of evil means—that made me face the fact that I had been wrong in my optimism, and that a society cannot be brought into being by doing just the things which it is the very purpose of the intended society to abolish for ever.

Evil means cannot produce good ends for the plain reason that men and not measures are the *ultima ratio,* and that men become what their thoughts and actions, day by day, have made them. A change of direction in a society cannot take place automatically, by a kind of jump, in the manner, if that is the manner, of a biological mutation. Except in the case of conquest, it can take place only because men in the society—a majority, a minority, or even a single individual—wish it to take place, and have the power to make the wish effective. But men's wishes are not unconditioned. A man is a new man every second: what he thought and did a second ago has changed him.

70

His wishes are the wishes of his present nature, not of his former one. If he has taken absolute power over others albeit with the intention of abolishing all power over others, including his own, the continued exercise of power must itself preclude him, sooner or later, from desiring to abolish it. If he has decided to lie for the purpose of establishing a purer truth—and in lying I include all forms of censorship and all manipulation of people's minds—then if he lies long enough he will not only cease to take any interest in truth but will cease even to know what truth is. And this is not only because the strength of any habit is cumulative: it is also because the urge to power (of which lying is a mode) is so compulsive in human nature that if you once give it rein you will never curb it.

While, therefore, it is always possible, however rarely it may have happened, that weariness or old age or some sudden conversion might induce a dictator to abdicate, it is improbable to the verge of impossibility that a whole group, if once habituated to absolute control of a State, should suddenly wish it to wither away. Nor, in the kind of society we are considering, can a change of direction come from below, except in one circumstance ; for the majority will be conditioned to contentment or perhaps enthusiasm, and the political police will see to the rest. The barricades have gone for ever, consigned to the museum of history even more by the technique of mass manipulation—manipulation of men's hearts and minds—than by the physical omnipotence of machine-guns and bombers. Only if libertarian ideas could be made to penetrate with sufficient steadiness from without might a desire for change become really widespread : and if it were widespread enough it might become effective even in a police State, for the ruling group might think it wise to make concessions. So democracy, in our sense of the word, might begin.

Another objection may be raised, and of quite a different kind. If man cannot live by bread alone, it may be said, he certainly cannot live without bread : unless men have food and health and security as a basis, any full development of their humanity is, for the majority at least, impossible. I agree ; I have been saying it, in my own person or vicariously as a publisher, most of my adult life. "Very well then" continues my hypothetical objector "you are omitting in all this talk about Soviet communism the most important fact of all. In that whole vast area poverty and unemployment, the twin curses of a capitalist economy, have gone for ever. Isn't that, in terms of the actual daily life on which you are so fond of insisting, worth everything else put together? The crucial fact is that, as a result of the economic revolution, the Soviet people are happy—or those at any rate are" he will add if he is honest "who do not concern themselves with politics, or, if they do, are content to follow, in any matter of real importance, the party line."

I have no wish to make debating points in reply. So far, the Revolution has not bettered the general living standards of the Russian people to anything like the extent that communists claim : but that is no argument against Soviet communism (nor of course against socialism), for the heroic task of industrialisation inevitably involved a low output of consumer goods, especially with war always on the horizon and even though something rather less Spartan might have been possible if ruthless preoccupation with the future had been tempered by a little more concern for existing lives. Of greater importance is the consideration that under a totalitarian dictatorship there can be no guarantee that the working masses will ever get their fair share of the industrial product ; and as to security, there was no unemployment under Hitler either. But replies like those, even when they are valid, as some of them are, get nowhere near the heart of the matter ; and it may not merely be conceded, it must be insisted, that economic well-being and security are the essential prerequisites for a good life, and that in the modern world nothing but a planned economy can secure them. But that is an argument for socialism, not for what is called the communism of Soviet Russia.

It is on what you mean by a good life—a good life for *men*— that everything turns. Ignore altogether, if you wish, the millions of Russian citizens who have been killed or exiled or imprisoned or made to do forced labour during the last so many years : forget also that millions more may, for all we know, be suffering these things, or some of them, at this very moment. Consider only the others, and imagine that they are all secure and materially prosperous. But man, said Aristotle, is a political animal. He is that, and much more besides ; and Aristotle himself meant something far wider than we mean by the word political. Every man is potentially a political, creative, individual creature : his glory is independence and his birthright is spontaneity. I want to see the potentiality realised, the birthright accepted, the glory achieved. I want to see a race of *men*, not of domestic animals however "happy": of self-directing intelligences, not of anthropoid automatons who will do what they are told and think what others prescribe for them. And I say that any ideal pettier than this rests, in the last analysis, on contempt for humanity.

PART II

Meanwhile we must face the fact that the power of the Soviet Union and of the local communist parties, and their effectiveness in establishing values contrary to ours, are likely not to diminish but to increase. How can we best meet this rivalry? There is only one way: and that is to foster our own values wherever we have the power to do so, and to foster them not in the careless and half-hearted way in which we do things in times of peace, but with the single minded intensity of our struggle for survival in times of war. The word war must not be misunderstood. It is no Jehad that I am preaching: nor am I suggesting—and I hope I need not say it—that we should seek to impose our ideas by any kind of force, either physical or moral. I simply mean that we must *live* our values uncompromisingly wherever we come into contact, individually or collectively, with other peoples, and particularly in our relation with those peoples. It is unnecessary to add that we can hardly do this effectively if we meanwhile betray these same values here at home. In a word, we can meet an opposing way of life only by living our own. At the same time, we must do everything we can to ensure that other peoples really know what our way of life in fact is.

I

How do we apply all this in our direct relation with the Soviet Union? The importance of an appropriate behaviour cannot of course be exaggerated. For while we may not buy peace at the cost of what ultimately makes life itself desirable, to avoid war should be our all but final aim, since war is the all but final enemy of everything for which we stand: and the Soviet Union is the only country in the world today that could conceivably be held to have both the will and the power to wage aggressive war.

Has she the will? Nobody can know the real aims of Soviet foreign policy, nor how they may develop in the future. Indeed, that way of putting it is altogether too simple; there are no doubt conflicting tendencies among the top groups in post-war Russia, and the dominant tendency at any moment will be determined by a number of internal and external pressures. I would hazard the guess that at the present time the dominant group is thinking somewhat as follows. The post-war situation presents an ideal opportunity for pushing forward the boundaries of the Soviet Union, increasing her power and influence, and damaging her potential rivals. In one place she can win new territory, in another she can set up a satellite Government, in a third (as in the Danube region) she can force economic control, in a fourth (as in the case of France, with the sale of half a million tons of wheat at the request of the communist Minister, M. Thorez) she can strengthen the local communists by adroit manoeuvring of every kind. Meanwhile she can take the utmost advantage of British difficulties by seeking to discredit us in every danger-spot throughout the world, and can make a special appeal to the colonial and emergent peoples, particularly in the Middle and Far East. Finally she can try, though so far without success, to divide us from America.

Is this or is it not a policy of imperialist expansion, not in the Leninist but in the good old-fashioned Spanish or British or French or German sense? I doubt whether it consciously either is or isn't; just as I doubt whether people are right when they say that Russia is thinking only of her own security. Surely the matter is simple enough. She is the rising nation or group of nations: she has innumerable opportunities for increasing her power: she seizes them, and waits to see what happens.

This push and thrust for power, moreover, is not merely "all mixed up" with a relentless drive towards world communism: it is essentially identical with that drive. People who imagine that Trotsky's exile meant the final defeat of "Trotskyism" are without the smallest understanding of communist dynamics. Events like that, or like the more recent "dissolution" of the Comintern, are mere incidents: temporary manœuvres, manœuvres of a few years or even of a generation or so, on the vast scale of world history. Whether they are instinctive or deliberate—and they are sometimes one and sometimes the other —is irrelevant. From its very nature Soviet communism *must* be a world movement: the controversy over "socialism in one country " was essentially no more than a quarrel about methods, intensified by personal rivalries. If communist loyalty is no longer to the Internationale, but that of communists inside Russia to the Soviet national anthem and that of communists outside Russia partly to this and partly to their own national anthems, the overriding purpose, though sometimes unconscious, remains the same. All that has happened is that the spearhead of the internationalism has itself become nationalist.

However all that may be, the present Soviet policy in international affairs must clearly involve the risk of war, and this is something of which Russia cannot be unaware. I am sure that she doesn't desire war ; but I am almost as sure that she doesn't contemplate it with the horror that we and the Americans feel at such a possibility. To begin with, there is still at the back of her mind the fixed Marxist tenet that sooner or later the final show-down between the socialist and the capitalist world is inevitable : and next, a war of atom bombs in say four or five years' time would damage her far less than ourselves, who would be more or less wiped out, and considerably less than the United States of America. And there is something further. We think with agony of the destruction of human life : she does not. I am not speaking bitterly, but stating what I believe to be a fact, when I say that for the Soviet Union men, and even her own men, are for the time being so much State material, whereas for us and the Americans men, or at least our own men, are always individual human souls. The reason for this is not only the communist view of means, though that contributes. The reason is also that in Russia, as in several countries of the East, human life has always been " cheap ", by no means because of anything peculiar in Russian or eastern " blood ", but because the tradition that human life is sacred has never yet, for historical and environmental reasons, taken firm root among them.

So that I think that Mr. Churchill was not far out when he said that the Soviet Union wants not war but the fruits of war. Hitler definitely wanted war ; and Stalin, for all the similarity in many of his international methods, isn't Hitler.

On any showing, however, the situation is perilous. How then should we act ? Questions such as that of the atom bomb, or oil, or the control of the Mediterranean would take me too far afield ; but the destruction of mental barriers, and from both sides, comes properly within my scope. That, which by no means implies "appeasement", is what we should pursue; and we should pursue it as energetically as we can, always provided that it is not bought on our side, as it certainly will not be bought on Russia's, by any betrayal of principle. Two aspects of the matter must be considered, though far more briefly than their importance demands.

§ 1

First, then, we must feel and show the maximum of tolerance. This does not for a moment mean that we should fail to protest when men in Berlin or anywhere else are kidnapped from their homes: on the contrary, we cannot protest too passionately. We protest, because these things are illiberal. But while we are intolerant of the acts, we must not be intolerant of the men who do them: for to be so would be to violate the very code against the breach of which we are protesting, since tolerance of persons is the essence of liberalism. Respect for personality demands that, having condemned the act, we should put ourselves in the actor's position: we should imagine ourselves as influenced by his history, moulded by his environment, subject to his impulses, dominated by his thought. It will save us from self-righteousness, too, if we reflect that time out of number we as a people have committed similar outrages, though less frequently of late, and that the original impulse of the communist philosophy, which has issued in so many things we detest, was far finer than some if not most of the motives that rule our daily lives. The very intensity of our devotion to liberal values, the very compulsion we feel to refute whatever thought and oppose whatever deed may violate them, imply a wholehearted tolerance of the men who think the thoughts and do the deeds. And it is specially necessary to be tolerant of those who are intolerant, as the Russians are intolerant, of us: for tolerance of the intolerant is the criterion of tolerance, just as respect for our enemies is the criterion of respect.

The tolerance for which I am pleading, while demanded absolutely and without further consideration by our liberalism, must, if that liberalism is indeed a correct response to reality and an act of cooperation with it, result of necessity in healthy consequences. It will so colour our thought that, while standing firm on every ground of principle, we shall quite automatically avoid the provocation in phrase or the pin-prick in policy which must increase intolerance on the other side, and so lead eventually to mutual hatred. And because in the contacts of mind and character the positive evokes the positive and the negative the negative, our tolerance will diminish the intolerance of those, however few they may be so long as Russia insists on impregnable barriers against general intercourse, who experience it.

Tolerance, though it requires no justification but itself, will come more easily to us if we know the history and understand the philosophy of those with whom we have to deal. We cannot imagine ourselves as influenced by a man's history unless we know that history; we cannot see ourselves as dominated by his thought unless we understand that thought. Nothing, therefore, is more important than an increasing familiarity with Russian history, and a wider study of Marxism both in its origins and in its development.

Most important of all, perhaps, is a thorough knowledge of the relations between Russia and the rest of the world since the Revolution of 1917. There is, no doubt, a great deal of stupid and one-sided talk about Russian suspicions. Her fear of Anglo-American designs is certainly not the sole incentive for her present expansionism, though it is probably a strong element in her complex of motives; and the Allied intervention of 1918-1922 cannot be an eternal justification, on the ground of suspicion and in the name of security, for any Russian act that may threaten the peace of the world. Though everything can and should be forgiven, history cannot be understood if half of it is forgotten: and half of it in this case, to speak only of the immediate past, is the tortuousness of Soviet negotiations with us in the summer of 1939, the Nazi-Soviet Pact, the rape of Poland, the attack on Finland, and the diplomatic and material support for Hitler from 1939 to 1941. But the other half must also be remembered: for instance the intervention of 1918-1922, the almost continuous record of diplomatic discourtesy, Soviet exclusion from Munich, the tortuousness of our negotiations with Russia in the summer of 1939, and the open declaration by at least one of our statesmen in 1940 that Russia ought to be attacked. Worst of all were the attitude and policies of Mr. Neville Chamberlain: for while I do not for a moment believe that he positively desired war between Germany and the Soviet Union, or incited Hitler to this course, he undoubtedly believed till early 1939 that it might, all in all, be best to allow Hitler to explode somewhere, and that if it was to be somewhere it had better be in the East. We must understand the effect of all this on Russian minds, however little they may understand the effect of the Pact on ours.

There is something else that we should do well to keep steadily in mind, if we are to preserve our sense of proportion. The Russian Revolution was one of the supreme events in human history. Everyone, I suppose, would agree with that statement: for no one would deny that something happened on a single day in 1917 which was in a peculiar sense decisive. History, of course, is made by every event and even every thought that may occur at any time anywhere in the world. For all that, she has her turning points, comparable with the moments (if there are such moments) which decisively herald the arrival of a new biological species. The Russian Revolution was one of those turning points. It may prove to have been a turning point for evil and it may prove to have been a turning point for good; and which it does prove to have been largely depends on us. For the Revolution, like Shelley's wild west wind, drove two ideas over the universe; the idea of economic socialism and the idea of totalitarian organisation and control. The totalitarianism is wholly evil: the economic socialism is potentially of incalculable good. It can " quicken a new birth "; but it can do so only if it is divorced from the totalitarianism and put to the service of liberal values. The idea of economic socialism—the idea that a nation's economy should be planned for the material welfare of the common people and not manipulated for the private advantages of the few—already, of course, existed: but the Revolution gave it an actuality and impetus impossible to exaggerate. The impetus remains, irrespectively of whether Russia herself can ever fully achieve, under totalitarianism, true socialism even in this purely economic sense. I am very doubtful about that; for the interests of controlling groups clearly *can* intervene still more effectively in a totalitarian régime of any kind than in a capitalist society of the " bourgeois-democratic " type. Nor need I emphasise at this stage that economic planning, even when it really and unreservedly is for the material welfare of the common people and even when it really does result in a high level of material prosperity, is not in itself enough; for while personality is always, in average men and women, abominably outraged by want, it is outraged hardly less by well-fed serfdom. With these reservations, however—

and they are of pivotal importance—economic socialism can make one of the greatest of all possible contributions to human progress. It comes, then, to this. If totalitarianism conquers, and whether it embodies a socialist element or not, the Russian Revolution will turn out to have been of disastrously evil augury. But if, on the other hand, we can accelerate still further in the world the socialist impetus that Russia gave; if at the same time we can conquer her totalitarianism by our liberalism, even eventually, perhaps, in Russia herself; and if, as an indispensable condition, we can keep the foundations of western civilisation inviolate: then in that event, but in that event only, the Revolution will rank, at the ultimate reckoning, as on balance one of the crucially progressive events in the history of the world. That does not mean that we should condone the evil in it, as all thorough Marxists (though occasionally with reluctance) condone it, on the specious plea of "historical necessity" or by any similar kind of intellectual wickedness; and still less, if that be possible, does it mean that we ourselves should adopt or encourage similar methods, or methods remotely resembling them, for any reason whatsoever. The proviso, moreover—the "in that event only"—implies a question the final answer to which I for one would be very loth indeed to predict. But when all has been said, and however passionately we may desire that the same result should have been achieved in a different manner, a recognition of even the possibility that the Russian Revolution may be seen generations ahead as one of the outstanding landmarks of human progress will help to save us from a fatal intolerance.

§ 2

Even the greatest tolerance, however, is of only limited value if contacts with the other party are lacking. Secondly, then, we should seize every opportunity of breaking down the barriers which divide our peoples from one another. The iron curtain, unlike most newspaper phrases, is a fact, though not quite in the sense in which the newspapers use it. Visits to Russia were permitted before the war, and increasingly, I should say, until war became imminent. The number, even at the freest period, was strictly controlled: great care was taken to exclude, whenever practicable, potential critics: but the door was always, or nearly always, open. Nor is it wholly true that visitors were prevented from going where they were not intended to go and seeing what they were not intended to see. For all that, any general intercourse between the peoples was, and was intended to be, impossible. Three devices prohibited it. First, almost every visitor was guided and toured; and anyone who has suffered from that mass indignity, either in Russia or elsewhere, knows that even when "free time" is on the programme curiosity is weaker than the desire to be alone. If nevertheless and in spite of the language difficulty an attempt was made to talk intimately with ordinary Russians, it was in general defeated, not so much by any positive prohibition as by the fear of contact with foreigners with which the Russian people had been deliberately inspired. Secondly, Russians were prevented, except in the rarest circumstances, from travelling abroad. Finally, there was more than a mere misreporting from time to time of particular events in foreign countries: there was a sustained campaign, by speech, by Press, by books, by every form of propaganda, to paint such a picture of western life and institutions as would make them grotesque and odious to Russian eyes. Similar distortions, this time of Soviet life, have been frequent, of course, in the baser part of the British Press. We all remember stories about the communisation of women. But there is a vital difference, not in intention, but in effect. In a totalitarian country, where every form of expression is controlled by the State, the truth cannot get through: in Britain, however slowly and however partially, it can.

It is not easy to formulate proposals for breaking down this barrier, since everything depends on willingness from the Russian side. A beginning has been made by publishing "The British Ally," and, in a small way, by broadcasting. It can only be said that there must be an unremitting effort on our part, however great and however steady the discouragement, to establish contacts of every kind—by exchange, for instance, of students and scientists, by getting what publications we can into Russian hands, and, best perhaps of all, by seizing every opportunity for joint work, from the lowest level to the highest, on international commissions. I do not pretend that all this will achieve very much: for it is that whole vast population of the Soviet Union, the 180 or 200 million and not a few odd hundreds or thousands, that will decide, or, the fear is, fail to decide the issue. The worst horror of the iron curtain is not that we don't know what is happening in Russia, disastrous though this is: the real tragedy is that the Russian masses not only do not know how other peoples think or live, but are deliberately persuaded that their thoughts and lives are something very different from what in fact they are. Unless this iron curtain can be effectively penetrated any hope of a firmly based understanding seems a chimaera ; and to find ways and means of penetrating it should be one of the most urgent tasks of British statesmanship.

II

I come now to the heart of what I want to say. Let me repeat that we must foster our values wherever we come into contact with other peoples, and particularly in our relation with those peoples. That brings me to Germany, about which I want to write for the remainder of this essay : by no means because other countries, such as Austria and Italy, are not of the greatest importance in this connection, but because it is in Germany above all that the Soviet Union and the West are counterpoised, and because, also, the fate of Germany will decide, or very largely decide, the fate of Europe and perhaps the world.

§ 1

Matters of machinery and technique will be dealt with later. All that need be said here is that we have failed in such matters. No one would under-estimate the difficulties : but in the control of our own zone in Germany we have had no clear strategy for the support of democratic elements or encouragement of democratic institutions. A great deal of good or at the very least well-meaning work has been done, in a patchy kind of way, by men on the spot ; but a comprehensive plan and a clear directing sense of final aims and detailed methods have been missing. It is true that the decisions of Yalta and Potsdam— the alienation of territory, the expulsion of populations, the divi-ion into zones, above all the criminal policy of de-industrialisation —had already made the creation of a genuine democracy any-where in Germany infinitely difficult. In so far as our statesmen sponsored or willingly acquiesced in these policies they bear a responsibility for which history will find it hard to forgive them ; and in so far as they yielded to pressure, they failed to understand that wickedness committed in the name of Allied unity may indeed be the pleasantest way at the moment, but must in due course bring its nemesis of intolerable suffering, and end by splitting the Allies themselves. It is true also that these policies, by their very nature, made Soviet methods in any part of Germany far easier, and western methods far more difficult. Yet when all has been said, the contrast between the Russian administration of their zone and our administration of ours has been startling. The Russians have known exactly what they wanted, and no less exactly how to get it. Their policy for land and industry ; their carefully calculated mixture of ruthlessness and leniency ; their "liquidation" of some Nazis, employment of others, and "re-education" of still others into communists ; and above all such a manipulation of the various parties that in the end the communists must be in absolute control—policies such as these have all been converging on one steadily envisaged end. By contrast, our own failure has been almost complete.

I wish first, however, to speak of something more fundamental.

§ 2

They have suffered, these Germans, an appalling spiritual catastrophe. Forget for a moment their responsibility ; or rather remember it, for in the case of those who are really responsible the responsibility is part, indeed the major part, of the catastrophe. For twelve years some of them have tyrannised and some of them have lived under tyranny. During all that period, a sustained appeal has been made to everything most base in human nature —in the human nature that is ours as well as theirs : to greed and lust for power, to self-interest, to that wretched nationalism which is a mode of personal glorification, to cruelty and pitilessness, and to the sado-masochistic instinct for ruling and being ruled. In particular, the minds of children have been subjected to a horrible malpractice ; they have been made to believe, in their helplessness, that good is evil and evil good. And then, with the coming of the war, some of them have sunk deeper and deeper into the mood of violence, and nearly all of them have suffered the further corruption which any war, even what is called a just war, inevitably brings : or brings, rather, to all but those (and they are nowhere very many) who, being pure in heart, are capable of spiritual resistance. Finally doubt, defeat, ruin and despair ; and a whole people, "good" or "bad," soldiers or peasants, old women or children, Nazi, non-Nazi or anti-Nazi, a target for the contempt and hatred of the civilised world.

Were their minds, or the minds of some of them, ready for the poison before Hitler came? Were they, or some of them, weak in their resistance to his coming? I little care. These questions are irrelevant, or rather they are relevant, so to speak, the other way. In both events there is all the more need for healing: if their minds were ready, because the corruption is of longer standing; and if they were weak, because an evil outside your control degrades you less than an evil you might, if you had been strong enough, have prevented. Most of all in need of healing are those who ordered or committed abominations, or approved of their commission, and are unrepentant; they are most in need of healing because they are unrepentant. I often read in sermons and letters to the Press on this subject that repentance must precede forgiveness (and forgiveness simply means, as between man and man, wishing the other well). and that while we might do well to forgive the repentant, to forgive the unrepentant would be immoral and irreligious. People who talk like that confuse the prerogative of God with the duty of man. It may be that God requires repentance before He will forgive: not being in His confidence, as so many appear to be, I cannot know. A theologian would perhaps say that the act of repentance and the act of forgiveness are the same act, being simultaneous modes of reconciliation. However that may be, for a man to set himself up and say "I will forgive you, if you repent" is to break the third commandment, and to take the name of the Lord our God in vain.

Here then is a whole people in a state of spiritual ruin such as has never been known, perhaps, in the history of the world. I presume that we wish to foster among them liberal thought, liberal practice and liberal institutions. They are geographically, and in some other ways, the navel of Europe. In the moral crisis that faces us, they can become, with whatever difficulty, a source of strength to western values; and they can become, very easily, the opposite. It must be the one or the other: there is no third possibility. The fundamental battle in Europe today is between the liberal way of thought and life, and those totalitarian ideas and institutions of which Soviet communism is now the strongest exponent. If liberalism vanishes from the heart of Europe, the battle for western civilisation is all but lost.

What fundamentally, we have to ask, has happened to this people? The answer is quite simple: circumstances have weakened in them, to a pitiable degree, the respect for personality—the personality of ourselves as well as of others—which is both the root and the flower of western civilisation. As the result of suggestion and instruction and inculcation, of an appeal to their instinct of self-interest and hatred and not to their instinct of cooperation and love, of the thoughts they have been made to think and the things they have been made to do, some of them have forgotten, and some have never known, that men, all men, are spiritual creatures, with the right and responsibility to be free. Kindness, which issues from respect, is nothing, they have been taught, but weakness; mercy and pity and forgiveness, which are its crown, are wickedness or folly. And every act of violence they have committed, every act of aggression in which they have been however indirectly involved, has made it easier for them to learn their lesson. Only one thing was wanting, and it was quickly added. The world loathed them in their defeat; and pariahs do not commonly respect either themselves or others.

I am far from suggesting that every German has suffered the spiritual degeneration that I have described. Too many brave and gentle and saintly Germans have allowed me, both before and after defeat, to know their hearts and minds for any such error to be conceivable. I believe, too, that when history tells the truth (if ever again, when there is such a decay of objectivity, she can) we shall know that the number of those who suffered and died for their liberal convictions is greater even than the most optimistic of us had ever dared to imagine. A Peer once wrote at the end of a little pamphlet, very famous in its day, that the honour laid on the men and women of this island in their fight against Hitler, the honour of "sharing Christ's sacrifice," was "far greater than any German could ever dream": but now they are putting up posters in Westphalia to combat resurgent fascism, and setting out on them how many ministers of religion and labour leaders were arrested or killed by the Nazis, and how many men and women of Westphalia were imprisoned in concentration camps.* Many of these people have survived, and the Minister responsible for German affairs said the other day in the House of Commons that men and women of democratic mind were now coming forward in good numbers. But it is the general climate that I have been attempting to describe ; and I have not done so, I think, unfairly. Nor do I write to criticise : in the face of such calamities judgment is silent, and pity takes the stand.

Now however violent and however widespread may have been the immediate reaction against the Hitlerism that had brought them to disaster, and with whatever sincerity the more politically conscious may have determined and may still determine to be done once and for all not only with Hitlerism but with every species of totalitarian tyranny, it is as clear as the day that unless the whole spiritual atmosphere can be changed there must be, even in the quite short run, an almost irresistible tendency away from liberalism. The habits of thought to which, in the mass, they have grown accustomed, and the features of character which have become dominant in them, will tell far more either than a mere temporary revulsion at the experience of defeat or than the efforts of a minority, even if wholeheartedly encouraged from without, to lead them towards democracy. Unless, I repeat, the climate can be changed the pull must be quite inevitably to systems based, not on respect for personality, but on the reverse : not to democratic and humanistic socialism, but to a resurgent fascism, to neo-fascism in one or other of its many forms, or to the present thought and practice of Soviet communism. Even if no magnet were there the movement would still be away from the West ; but when Soviet communism is in the field can it be doubted where, in the absence of a psychological transformation, the victory must eventually lie? The fact that the majority of Germans still prefer us to the Russians, though not quite so strongly as before, is of little importance, and so is the defeat of communists for the time being at elections outside the Russian zone : what matters is that Soviet communism has a way of life to offer which Germans, however little they themselves may realise it, have been conditioned over long years to accept. The Berlin communists were not so wrong when they said in 1931 "after Hitler, us ". Add to the credit account of the communists their idealism, their single-mindedness, their sense of vocation, their religious lack of scruple, their dominating leadership, their appeal to nationalist sentiment, their cry for "German unity," and their determination to win the soul not only of Germany but of all Europe, and you have the picture complete.

Can we effect the psychological transformation? Can we make them, not so much understand as remember in the sense in which Plato used the word, that in respect for personality is life and being, but in contempt for others, any others, death and nothingness? Can they see mercy, with Milton, as throned in celestial sheen: or pity, with Blake, as a virtue of delight? Can they, through what we say and think and do, realize that all mistreatment, for whatever end, is a sin against the Rights of Man? Can they long for everybody's freedom? And can they feel these things, not as passing gusts of emotion, but with the inner certainty and conviction that changes the whole course of a man's life? Perhaps most important of all, can they be won, in this crisis of their fate, to self-reliance, self-direction and self-respect?

If they can, the struggle for western values in Germany will still be immensely hard: our encouragement of democratic institutions and economic reconstruction will still have to be as determined and single-minded as the Russian manœuvres for communist supremacy: but there will be reasonable hope of a successful issue. If they cannot, there can be no hope at all.

I am sure that we can bring this change. It is the one thing, in the political world of today, of which I am completely sure. I am sure of it because every bit of experience of myself and others, all the lessons of marriage and parenthood and no matter what kind of personal intercourse, tell me that there is one method which, in the very nature of spiritual reality, can never fail. When Christ told us to do good unto them that despitefully use us and to pray for them that curse us that we may be children of our Father which is in heaven, he was not inventing a method of behaviour which he thought might have satisfactory results: he was making a statement about reality. And every one of us knows in his heart, however bitterly our baser instincts may fight against the knowledge, that the statement is a true one. Evil evokes evil, and good good; and good, if it is strong enough, overcomes evil.

If we treat these Germans kindly, kindness will stir in them. If we show them mercy, they will know, by the immediacy of contact, how "delightful" mercy is. If we, the enemy, act justly to them when we could have acted unjustly—if we give them the rights that we might so easily have withheld—then they will understand what rights mean, just because we had the power to withhold them. And if we respect them—all of them, whatever some may be or may have done, for such considerations cannot modify respect in the sense I am insisting on—respect, by some process of mutuality, will be born in them, not only for us but for themselves and others. Martin Büber tells somewhere how, as he was looking into his dog's eyes, there was suddenly, for the fraction of a second, complete and immediate—unmediated—recognition, not the one of the other, but between them. That is how these things work. I do not mean, of course, that a change in the temper of the German people can be a matter of days or weeks: a boy who has been indoctrinated for twelve years with Nazism does not become a liberal or a Christian overnight. Nor can it be accomplished easily or by the way. The very depth of the moral wound requires a corresponding intensity in the effort to reach and cure it. Only if we feel the same passionate devotion to our ethic as Hitler felt for his and the communists feel for theirs, and only if we apply it with complete integrity and sustained consistency where in human weakness we might fail to apply it but where by the same token its application is the criterion of our sincerity—only so can we win the heart of Germany and ultimately, perhaps, of the whole world. And why should we lack passion? Isn't it as good, this way of life that has produced so much gentleness and so many freedoms, as the barbarism of Hitler and the ruthless expediency of what is now called communism?

I shall be told, no doubt, that all this is mere sentimentality. It is odd how people misuse the word: they appear to mean by "sentimental" trying, if I may put it babyishly, to be good. Sentimentality, as I understand it, is insincerity in the feeling or showing of emotion: feeling or showing emotion that isn't real. But to obey our better instincts and deny the baser, in such small degree as we are able, is on the contrary to be not less real but more. What people usually mean when they condemn sentimentality is that they admire moral toughness: but moral toughness isn't virtue.

I shall also be told that I am forgetting security. The argument, if that is not too polite a word, of the "hold them down" school is sometimes that the Germans as such are militant and predatory, butcher-birds as Lord Vansittart called them, and will always make war unless they are forcibly prevented; and sometimes that any defeated nation thirsts for revenge, and must therefore be deprived of the means of achieving it. I propose to say nothing at all about the first argument: it is based on ignorance (at best) of psychology and science, and can be corrected in half an hour by reference to any textbook of European or world history. Its prevalence is due, of course, to the infection of Nazi racialism: and it is peculiarly distressing to find some of my fellow Jews, whose kin have suffered most from it, falling a victim to this poison. About the second argument four things may be said. First, it displays the mentality of those General Staffs who are always preparing to fight the previous war: with its hypnotised concentration on the last five minutes and a fraction of the world's surface it forgets that everything changes every day, and that a new war is produced, not by the circumstances that produced the last one, but by a situation resulting, after many years, from the continuous interplay of changing forces over the whole international field. (Which is not to deny that for a given period, such as the comparatively insignificant one of eighty years, a particular country may be the main storm-centre.) Secondly, this argument, like the first, ignores history: Austria did not thirst for revenge after Bismarck's settlement, nor South Africa after ours. If you give a defeated enemy cause for revenge, he will seek it; if not, not. France's case, or part of it, for annexing the Rhineland and the Ruhr is a gloss, as logically beautiful as it is morally repulsive, on the argument from revenge. By the annexation of her eastern territories, says France, you have made German hatred inevitable: she will clearly seek vengeance in the West: therefore, in the name of security, annex her western territories. And thereby, they might have added, make her will to vengeance doubly inevitable. I am not blaming France: given the absence of any vestige of internationalism, and with every country fighting for its own hand, there is a good deal in her case. I also think, as I shall show presently, that with things as they now are we must go very far indeed towards meeting French desires. But you might wonder, if you were thinking in terms of world politics, whether it wouldn't have been simpler to refrain from annexations altogether.

Isn't it really possible, in this matter of security, to abandon phrases detached from reality and devoid of any correspondence with the findings of history or intimations of commonsense—"seeing that they don't start it again", "making it impossible for them to renew their aggression", "disarming them permanently", "taking no risks"—and to consider instead the facts as we observe them and the probabilities that experience may foresee? No one could imagine that the Germany of this moment is a menace to anyone : whom is she to attack, and with what? The question is whether, as the years go on, Germans—men and women, concrete individuals like you and me, not "the Germans" or "Germany"—will desire peace or desire war, and, if they desire war, whether they will be able to make their desire effective. They will desire peace if their minds and hearts are peaceful, and war if otherwise ; and if they desire war, then sooner or later we shall certainly get it. How in the long run can you make seventy million people harmless, if they want to be harmful? In a static world of robots it might be possible : in the changing world of living men and women there is literally no way. The belief that Germany can or will be permanently "held down" is based on the singular delusion that we, and not only we but our children and our children's children, will all be thinking about the Germans and one another—we and the Russians and the Americans and the French and the Poles and the Czechs and so on as long as you like that we shall all be thinking in a year or five years or twenty or fifty precisely as we are thinking today. It would have been as reasonable to suppose, as apparently some people did suppose, that the United Nations would remain automatically united, or could be kept united by a mere piece of machinery and a paper constitution, when the particular circumstance that had united them in a common interest transcending, but for the time being only, their innumerable differences, namely Hitler's aggression, had passed into history. New hostilities will arise, as they are arising now before our eyes : the eternal flux will not be stayed ; and as generation succeeds generation each in turn will have known not Joseph. Our experience between the wars should have taught us this lesson. To take only the one case, our feeling for Germany, or the feeling of very many, varied between the extremes of intense dislike and warm sympathy : and a policy of astronomical reparations in 1919 was replaced, after only a few short years, by a policy of no reparations at all. The realists, who had advised us in the early twenties to squeeze Germany till the pips squeaked, were solemnly warning us in the early thirties that nothing could save us from Bolshevism but a strengthened Reich ; and men who had loudly insisted that Wilhelm should be hanged, and had felt cheated when he wasn't, were now preparing to hobnob with Hitler at the Nuremberg rallies. In 1919 "justice" demanded a "hard" peace, and anyone who refused to join in the clamour was a sentimental fool : but one of the main obstacles to an effective mobilisation of opinion against the Nazi menace a decade or so later was the growing feeling, not only in 1933 but in 1938, that Versailles was unjust and that Hitler couldn't be blamed for attacking it. In 1920, if my memory is not at fault, we still sang Wagner in English: in 1937 the typists were learning German.

Is not the real risk, therefore, that when, in a changing world, we may no longer have the will, or perhaps the power, to "hold Germany down": or when commercial self-interest, or the impact of her unemployed on our conscience, may prompt us to restore her industrial resources and right the balance of her economic life: or when the fact is faced, as faced it must be, that some measure of German prosperity—and there's the thin end of the wedge—is an indispensable condition for European recovery: or when, as new tensions develop, some Power may woo her or "build her up" or rearm her as a makeweight against some other Power that is now a rival but was once a friend—isn't the real risk that when these possibilities, and many more than can be easily foreseen, become actualities, there in the territories that command Europe will be men whose hearts desire aggression, and who will therefor aggress, or throw in their lot with some new aggressor, now that the road is open to them? Security will be assured, in so far as it can ever be assured, not by some dead piece of mechanics, not by some series of restrictions that will surely be relaxed directly circumstances have outdated them, but by so behaving, here and now, to those who might threaten our security that, when the time comes, they will have no wish to do so. So the road to peace and the road to that strengthening of western values of which I had been speaking are one: our ethic precludes aggression as well as totalitarianism, and we can win acceptance for that ethic, and so safeguard peace as well as liberalism, by practising it. If in our relations with the conquered we do justice and show mercy and walk humbly, not casually or when it suits us but with the intensity of conviction that Hitler showed for his ethic and the communists show for theirs, we can win Germany (or that part of it where, after so much damage has been done, we can still have any influence) both for liberalism and for peace.

§ 3

Has our behaviour been, is it now, of this pattern? Did we, as soon as the last shot was fired, show that Hitler's ways were not our ways, and that we cared enough for the faith we had defended to practise it—and that's the test—in our treatment of the enemy? On the contrary. Instead of doing justice and showing mercy and walking humbly, we did as Hitler would have done. We annexed, we expelled, we stole: we exhibited an extreme of nationalist intolerance: we bore ourselves with offensive superiority: when the pinch came, and the choice was between a little less comfort for ourselves and starvation for the enemy, we let them starve: and the twin bases of our policy were the secular wickednesses of self-interest, or what we grotesquely misunderstood as such, and *vae victis*. I am not suggesting, God forbid, that we did these things to the degree to which Hitler would have done them: if I thought that I should think the war fought in vain, which is very far from being the case. But we acted more in Hitler's spirit than in ours; and was this the way, I ask, to wean the German people from Hitlerism or the basic ideas of which Hitlerism is merely one expression? Was it not rather to convince them that all our liberal talk had been so much hypocrisy, that the war had been merely a trial of strength in which they happened to have lost, and that a ruthless selfishness was the norm of behaviour which everyone, when it came to it, adopted?

I say that "we" did all these things. I am aware that, with two exceptions, the worst of these outrages were committed jointly by the Allies, and that we, or rather our statesmen, were no more than a party to decisions of which, for all I know, they may have strenuously disapproved. They had to agree, it is sometimes said, first for the sake of victory and then to keep the Allies united. Well, if this plea is valid it is valid also for such of those now or recently on trial in various parts of Germany, and they are many, who can as justly plead that they too acted under duress. But it is not valid. Victory was as much the interest of our Allies as of ourselves: and our refusal to adopt policies which must make a mock of victory would have been no more likely to imperil victory than their pressure to adopt them. Nor can we escape by claiming that the responsibility is at worst our statesmen's and not ours. In a democratic country statesmen cannot act in defiance of public opinion, if it is sufficiently strong and adequately vocal. The facts were soon known. Where was the outcry, the passion of disapproval? On the contrary, the majority either cared nothing or approved.

I am aware, also, that the day by day administration of

the British zone, for all the fatal deficiencies of which I shall speak at the end of this essay, has been far more decent than that of any other, and that many of our men on the spot have acted in accordance with our best traditions. But such qualifications, welcome though they are, can do little to modify the all-over situation, whether in the British zone or elsewhere. They are oases in a vast desert of wrong-doing. Touches of enlightenment there may be, but they are painted on a dark background of injustice and spoliation, of self-interest and superiority; and it is these attitudes of her conquerors, and their adding now of intensified hunger to spiritual despair, that must determine the mind and heart of post-war Germany—unless, from our side, there is a change of direction. But time is desperately short.

If anyone thinks that I exaggerate it is because he shuts his eyes to the facts. When men recover, if they ever do recover, their objectivity, Yalta and Potsdam will be names of infamy; and what will be remembered will be, not the photographs of Mr. Churchill and President Roosevelt and Marshal Stalin in smiling good-fellowship, but decisions which brought unutterable wretchedness to millions and will bring it to many more, and which sooner or later must divide the men, or their countries, which were jointly responsible. And sooner, not later. I need not have gone back to what people said in 1919 and 1933 respectively for an illustration of the speed with which, in the international field, men eat their words and reverse their policies. There is a more recent example; and the interval is shorter. "I cannot accept the view" said Mr. Churchill in the House of Commons on December 15th 1944 "that the arrangements which have to be proposed about the frontiers of the new Poland are not solid and satisfactory. . . The Poles are free, so far as Russia and Great Britain are concerned, to extend their territory, at the expense of Germany, to the West. I do not propose to go into exact details, but the extensions, which will be supported by Britain and Russia, bound together as they are by the 20 years' Alliance, are of high importance. . . The transference of several millions of people would have to be effected from the East to the West or North, as well as the expulsion of the Germans—because that is what is proposed: the total expulsion of the Germans—from the area to be acquired by Poland in the West and North. For expulsion is the method which, so far as we have been able to see, will be the most satisfactory and

93

lasting. . . I am not alarmed by the prospect of the disentanglement of populations, nor even by these large transferences, which are more possible in modern conditions than they ever were before. . . . Nor do I see why there should not be room in Germany for the German populations of East Prussia and of the other territories I have mentioned." Mr. Churchill returned to the theme two months later. "In supporting the Russian claim to the Curzon line" he said on February 27th 1945 "I repudiate and repulse any suggestion that we are making a questionable compromise or yielding to force or fear, and I assert with the utmost conviction the broad justice of the policy upon which, for the first time, all the three great Allies have now taken their stand. Moreover, the three Powers have now agreed that Poland shall receive substantial accessions of territory both in the North and in the West." Then comes a passage repulsive in its cynicism—I am sorry to say it, for my gratitude to Mr. Churchill transcends all other feelings—and heartbreaking for its folly. "We need not fear" he continued "that the task of holding these new lines will be too heavy for Poland, or that it will bring about another German revenge, or that it will, to use a conventional phrase, sow the seeds of future wars. We intend to take steps far more drastic and effective than those that followed the last war, because we know much more about this business, so as to render all offensive action by Germany utterly impossible for generations to come." There, in those two short sentences, and distilled to its finest essence, you have that combination of turpitude and folly which is driving the world to an ever deepening catastrophe. Commit an act of gross injustice, says Mr. Churchill: the victims will thirst for revenge, but that cannot matter, for we are "taking steps" to nullify the result "for generations". Is turpitude too strong a word? And "for generations", he implies, the three great Allies will still be embracing one another, and "Britain" and "Russia" and "America" will be thinking precisely as they think on February 27th 1945. Could folly be greater? Only a year was to elapse before Mr. Churchill himself, as if to point the moral, would be saying at Fulton, when he threw down his challenge to the Soviet Union, "The Russian-dominated Polish Government has been encouraged to make enormous and wrongful inroads upon Germany, and mass expulsions of millions of Germans on a scale grievous and undreamed of are now taking place." But Mr. Churchill did not merely dream of these expulsions: he sanctioned and defended them.

III

It is difficult to speak calmly of these decisions of Yalta and Potsdam. They may be summed up in four words: annexation, expulsion, spoliation, and economic enslavement; all of which, it may be remembered, are among the main counts of the Nuremberg indictment. Germany's historic eastern lands, where her people had lived and toiled for generations, and which had been her richest food-producing areas, were torn from her and placed under alien domination. There was no suggestion, however hypocritical, that justice either demanded this dictate or might in some measure condone it; and hypocrisy would have been welcome, for it would have shown that a certain standard of decency was at least still recognised, if nevertheless disobeyed. Justice, hypocritically or otherwise, simply did not come into the matter. You will find quite clearly exposed, in one of those statements by Mr. Churchill that I have quoted, the open cynicism of the whole transaction. Russia wanted East Prussia: she also wanted Poland (here there was a case in justice) up to the Curzon line: Poland must therefor be "compensated" "at the expense of" Germany. These words "compensated" and "at the expense of" occur time after time in the debates of that period. All that mattered was that a bargain should be struck between Poland and Russia: Germany existed only as a convenient means for striking it. What the Germans might feel, what the effect might be on the lives of themselves and their children, was more than merely irrelevant: it did not even come into the sphere where relevancy or otherwise is so much as considered. The Germans had been conquered: they had no rights. That was all there was to it.

One piece of pretence there was. While East Prussia was definitely to be annexed by the Soviet Union, the final destination of the other alienated lands was not to be decided, we were told, till the Peace Treaty. It was a miserable pretence, and only a very backward schoolboy, or a half-witted politician, could have been deceived by it. Meanwhile, the Poles were to be not merely permitted but encouraged to expel the German population from its homes, so as to put beyond any possibility of doubt the permanence of the Polish tenure.

*　　*　　*　　*

If the conscience of men ever again becomes sensitive, these expulsions will be remembered to the undying shame of all who committed or connived at them. Some fourteen million Germans in all, including those from Cechoslovakia, were, or were to be, involved; and it may be added, since many appear to assume that an adult man has no heart to feel or nerves to suffer, that the majority were women and old men and children. Potsdam "suggested" or "recommended"—I forget the precise word, and have no interest to look it up—that the expulsions, which had already started, should be carried out "in an orderly and humane manner." Here at any rate was a welcome piece of lip-service to humanity. But it could be, and I am afraid, in the absence of any plans and arrangements for implementing the proviso, was intended to be, lip-service only. The inevitable happened. Potsdam was taken as a signal to go ahead: the "suggestion" or "recommendation" was ignored. It was more than ignored. The Germans were expelled, not just with an absence of over-nice consideration, but with the very maximum of brutality.

I am told that readers do not care for long quotations. Well, whether they care for them or not I am going to print a whole series. If you are sickened or surfeited by them, so much the better; fourteen million human beings had and have to endure these things, not merely read about them:

The Potsdam announcements are still bringing repercussions from all parts of the world. Perhaps the fullest welcome is given in Poland and Czechoslovakia. The Governments of both countries assume that their plans for expelling several million Germans from their territories have been completely accepted.

The Times, August 7th, 1945.

Here, for instance, is what happened last month in Brno when young revolutionaries of the Czech National Guard decided to "purify" the town.

Shortly before 9 p.m. they marched through the streets calling on all German citizens to be standing outside their front doors at nine o'clock with one piece of hand luggage each, ready to leave the town for ever.

Women had ten minutes in which to wake and dress their children, bundle a few possessions into their suitcases, and come out on to the pavement. . . . Then they were marched out of town at gun-point towards the Austrian border.

It was pitch dark when they reached the border. The children were wailing, the women stumbling. The Czech border guards pushed them over the frontier towards the Austrian border guards.

Then more trouble started. The Austrians refused to accept them; the Czechs refused to readmit them. They were pushed into a field for the night, and in the morning a few Rumanians were sent to guard them.

They are still in that field, which has been turned into a concentration camp. They have only the food which the guards give them from time to time. They have received no rations.

A typhus epidemic now rages among them, and they are said to be dying at the rate of 100 a day.

Twenty-five thousand men, women and children made this forced march from Brno. . . . Even German Jews and anti-Nazis recently released from Gestapo concentration camps are not immune; neither are British women married to Germans.

Rhona Churchill (with U.S. Third Army), Daily Mail, August 6th.

BERLIN, August 7th. Between 12,000,000 and 14,000,000 Germans already on the move or who will have to move from the eastern parts of Germany, now under Polish or Czech control, are causing a gigantic refugee problem in Germany. They are mostly old people, women and children. . . .

Refugees said that the Poles give people thirty minutes to depart. In Danzig evictions take place street by street.

The Times, August 8th.

Under the bomb-wrecked roof of the Stettiner Railway Station —the Euston or King's Cross of Berlin—I looked this afternoon inside a cattle truck shunted beside the buffers of No. 2 platform.

On one side four forms lay dead under blankets on cane and raffia stretchers; in another corner four more, all women, were dying.

One, in a voice we could hardly hear, was crying out for water.

Sitting on a stretcher, so weakened by starvation that he could not move his head or his mouth, his eyes open in a deranged, uncomprehending stare, was the wasted frame of a man. He was dying, too.

As I walked about the station a score of others came up to me, all ravenous and starved, for whom also, like those in the cattle-truck mortuary, nothing could be done—until death.

Two women sanitary helpers did what they could in ministering to the small wants of the dying.

The train from Danzig had come in. It had taken seven days on the journey this time; sometimes it takes longer.

Those people in the cattle truck, and hundreds who lay on bundles of belongings on the platform and in the booking hall, were the dead and dying and starving flotsam left by the tide of human misery that daily reaches Berlin, and next day is turned back to take train to another town in a hopeless search of food and succour.

Thousands more—up to 25,000 in a day—trek on foot to the outskirts of Berlin, where they are stopped and forbidden entry to the already overcrowded city.

Each day between fifty and 100 children—a total of 5,000 already over a short period—who have lost both parents, or have been abandoned, are collected from Berlin's stations and taken to orphanages or found foster-mothers in Berlin.

That is all that Berlin charity can do.

For this problem at the moment is the Germans' own; the Allies have made no move to render relief or even give the Social Welfare Organisation, with its staff of thirty-three and 220 helpers all told, any assistance whatever.

Without any central control (no telephone lines or cars are put at the organisation's disposal, and the only means of co-ordinating any plan, even if it existed, is by occasional cycle courier at the mercy of sympathetic military road controls) the Welfare Committees are trying to grapple with a problem that is beyond their powers.

Here in Berlin we are living under this shadow, not just of hunger and want, but of death, and epidemics on a scale that the world has not seen in recorded history.

The expulsion of Germans from Polish-occupied Germany east of the Oder, and the mass transfers of population into the provinces of Pomerania, Mecklenburg, Brandenburg and Saxony, are projecting a tragedy of the greatest magnitude. It is almost already out of hand.

At a conservative estimate—given me by Dr. Karl Biaer,

anti-Nazi, now installed as head of Berlin's Social Welfare Committee—there are 8,000,000 homeless nomads milling about the areas of the provinces around Berlin.

If you take in the Sudeten Germans expelled from Czechoslovakia and those on the move from elsewhere the figure of those for whom no food can be provided rises to 13,000,000 at least. . . .

What is aggravating the problem beyond all solution is the continuation by the Poles of the ejection of German nationals from their homes, literally at a moment's notice.

This is in direct defiance of the Potsdam Declaration, which urged that the transfers of population must be carried out "in an orderly and humane manner."

A woman I met at the Stettiner Station had left Danzig on August 13th—eleven days after the standstill order was made. . . .

Other things I saw when the Danzig train came in I am bound to record. Apart from the women rocking in tears and anguish, and the famished children asleep in their arms or crying for food, there was a group of young men—all Poles—who sat apart, waiting for the next train to go out.

Then they would board it, and going through the train, would force these unprotected mothers and women to give up any possessions of value, including watches and jewels.

The guards on the train and at stopping places are shot if they attempt to intervene.

> Norman Clark (writing from Berlin),
> *News Chronicle,* August 24th.

One woman [among those seen at the Stettiner Station], emaciated, with dark rings under her eyes and sores breaking out all over her face, could only mutter self-condemnation because she was unable to feed her two whimpering babies. I watched her trying desperately to force milk from her milkless breasts—a pitiful effort that only left her crying at her failure.

> Charles Bray (writing from Berlin),
> *Daily Herald,* August 24th.

A typhoid epidemic is reaching such dimensions in Berlin that the medical authorities are gravely concerned. During the last four weeks the figures have risen from 358 cases in the week ending August 11th to 723 last week. . . .

This is yet another result of the mass expulsion of Germans

from Danzig, East Prussia and Poland. The refugees, infected and in an extremely low state of health, brought the disease with them. Conditions in Berlin were ideal for it to become rife throughout the city.

Charles Bray (writing from Berlin),
Daily Herald, September 8th.

One report, received a few days ago from a high dignitary of the German Church (for whose integrity and reliability your correspondent can vouch) says: "... I know the pains of the non-Ayrans. I did bear the tortures of the concentration camps, but what now happens before our eyes that is beyond everything that ever happened in form or extent. I am thinking of those taking their lives out of despair.

"Thousands and tens of thousands dying in the country roads by hunger and exhaustion. Thousands do not know since weeks and months where they will find an abode. Thousands are separated from their relations; children err [wander?] along; the parents shot [or] died are lost.

"When once, eight or nine years ago, dozens of non-Ayrans took their lives, I started for the Dutch Minister and begged him to entreat the Dutch Government to loosen the laws of immigration, to give those hopeless people a new hope. For God shall once challenge the souls of these poor driven to death also from us; and every Christian must feel himself guilty of these dying wretches, who see no other way in their despair than suicide. At every suicide Martha's words sound in my ear (John xi. 21): 'Lord, if Thou hadst been here, my brother had not died.'

"Now I beg for a new home for the children which are without parents, for the youth with no future, for those whose life is without hope. Venerable Bishop, set all your influence at the representatives of the Dominions in London, that to all these people a new home is given in the not occupied districts of the Dominions. Those folks driven by hunger and utmost necessity want to build themselves a new life through their hands' work, and they will be bearers of blessings and true guarantees of peace."

Manchester Guardian, September 8th.

Faced with this prospect of a disaster overwhelming a whole nation, the Allied public health authorities are ordering burgomasters to take measures ensuring the easy burial of the dead in the winter.

Graves are to be dug now which men debilitated by weeks of under-nourishment will not have the strength to dig in a few months' time. . . . Coffins will have to be dispensed with, what wood is available being needed for fuel. . . .

Death-rate for Berlin for the first month of the Allied Four-Power occupation was sixty-one per 1,000 of the population, against an expected figure of eleven or twelve. Of 609 new babies and infants under the age of one, 361 died.

Norman Clark (writing from Berlin),
News Chronicle, September 10th.

No reliable evidence is available of the number of evicted Germans who are passing through the Russian zone from the eastern frontier, but they probably run into millions, and in their desire to move to the west large numbers of them are coming up against the sealed frontiers of the British and American zones, which already have trouble enough on their hands.

The number of refugees passing through Berlin by train has apparently dropped from 20,000 to 10,000 a day, due, it is stated, to a decrease in the flow from the Sudetenland, but any discussion of this tragic problem is unreal until facts are produced about the extent to which the Poles have been allowed to clear German towns and villages in their forward surge to the Oder and the Neisse, which are expected to mark their new western frontier. The Potsdam Declaration, it will be remembered, called for the humane treatment of expelled German nationals, and in view of the distressing reports laid before the Conference from such cities as Breslau and Stettin, the countries concerned were urged to postpone further expulsions.

No evidence exists that these directives have been observed. In the Robert Koch Hospital here, which I visited this morning, there are more than sixty German women and children, many of whom were summarily evicted from a hospital and an orphanage in Danzig last month, and, without food and water or even straw to lie on, were dispatched in cattle trucks to Germany. When the train arrived in Berlin they said that of eighty-three persons crammed into two of the trucks twenty were dead.

A woman recovering from typhoid had, she stated, seen her husband beaten to death by Poles and she had then been driven from her farm near Danzig to work in the fields. Now she has survived the journey to Berlin with two young sons, and, without money, clothes or relations, cannot see what the future holds.

Three orphans I saw aged between eight and twelve are still almost skeletons after ten days' treatment, owing to the almost complete lack of fats in Berlin; none of them weighed more than three stone.

Another small boy turned out of Danzig had a scrawled post-card attached to him stating that his soldier father was long since missing and that his mother and two sisters had died of hunger.

It is surely not enough to say that the Germans brought these miseries upon themselves; brutalities and cynicism against which the war was fought are still rife in Europe, and we are beginning to witness human suffering that almost equals anything inflicted by the Nazis. There is an urgent need for complete information on these mass expulsions; all the control council could do to-day was to refer the subject to its co-ordinating committee for full study.

Berlin Correspondent of *The Times*,
writing on September 10th.

In one hospital he [J. B. Priestley] visited were the survivors of a Stettin orphanage who arrived in Berlin after a voyage in an overcrowded barge along canals, rivers and waterways. . . .

When a British officer went on board in the west port of Berlin he found the children's faces marked by starvation, scabies and sores.

Their bodies, legs and knees, swollen by hunger œdema—the typical attribute of starvation—were bitten by vermin. . . .

Mr. Priestley told me after visiting them: "What I have seen and heard from responsible relief workers on the spot shocks the conscience—and it would upset the conscience of anyone in England could they visit Berlin and see for themselves."

Norman Clark (writing from Berlin),
News Chronicle, September 12th.

At present it is almost impossible to find out in detail what is going on, but there is plenty of reason to doubt that the Potsdam clauses referring to humane conditions for the evacuation of these people are not being respected, at least by the Poles; though, on the other hand, following the recent disclosures, the Czech Government has modified its evacuation policy, a factor largely responsible for the drop in the average number of refugees arriving daily from 15,000 to 8,000.

In Danzig and elsewhere under Polish control it is believed

that the Germans are being rounded up on a house-to-house basis and marched off to railway stations with only the goods they can carry. All sorts of reports are current as to their fate on their way over the Oder. For example, at Küstrin one train-load of several hundreds was stopped, and, since typhus was raging amongst its occupants, were chased out into the fields by the German authorities lest they should enter the town, bringing with them contamination.

This may not be true. It may also not be true that nearly all the towns in the evacuation area have patrols out on the roads to intercept refugees and prevent them entering the area and sharing food rations already depleted by Russian requisitions. But there is no doubt that refugees arrive in Berlin in a horrible state—that can be seen by anyone who goes down to the Lehrter Bahnhof in the evening—and that once they have been sent forward from Berlin, where they can remain only twenty-four hours unless too ill to move, there is no check on what becomes of them. . . .

Most of these refugees are women and children.

Berlin Correspondent of *The Manchester Guardian*, writing on September 12th.

I am speaking on the basis of first-hand testimony. During my tour I visited Switzerland because it is the one country in Europe where you can meet officially trained investigators who are going to and from the war-racked countries. I was in Switzerland about a month and talked at length with people from all the central European countries. . . .

In the woods around Berlin corpses are hanging from the trees. Other men, women and children throw themselves into the rivers. Hundreds of corpses are continually drifting down the rivers Elbe and Oder. All the roads leading to Berlin are crowded with exiles. Thousands fall exhausted at the roadsides. Children may be seen trudging along pathetically without their parents. Hundreds of people are dying daily beside the roads from hunger and disease.

Rev. Henry Carter, *New Leader*, September 15th.

* * * *

That was what was happening in the high summer and early autumn of 1945. And it is happening, not, I hope and believe, on the same scale, and not now, in this matter of expulsions, from the side of the Czechs, but happening none the less as I write in the Spring of 1946. When millions were already on the road, efforts were made, too late for the thousands that were dead, to stop the expulsions and resume them only when arrangements for an orderly and humane evacuation had been completed. Our Government, and it is a pleasure to say it, took the lead in these negotiations. But that their success was very partial may be judged by this despatch from *The Manchester Guardian's* correspondent at Lübeck, writing on March 10th, 1946:

"In spite of the Potsdam agreement that the transfer of the German population from the East should be orderly and humane, the Polish authorities are evicting Germans from the newly acquired Polish territories with as little as ten minutes' notice and are sending them into the British zone without food in overcrowded trains.

"A man of 73 and a child of 18 months were found dead in the first transport which arrived in Lübeck under the 'Operation Swallow' scheme on March 3. The second transport had three dead. On the average 1,500 people are packed in trains of 26 coaches, which are unheated and for the most part damaged. The fourth transport brought 2,070 people, so that most had scarcely enough room to stand, much less sit.

"The British and Polish authorities agreed that the Poles should provide rations for a journey of two days, but scarcely any food is provided. On the first train each person received half a loaf of bread for the journey. On the second train a 3lb. loaf was divided among eight people, and a pound of sugar among 60. On the third train there was no food, only tea and hot water. These rations cover the journey only from Stettin to Lübeck, which lasts about 22 hours. But before the refugees reach the Stettin assembly point they often have to travel seven days, so that most have no real meal for ten days. They arrive at the transit camps exhausted or sick. In the first transport 350 people were ill, and 250 of them had to be taken to hospital in Lübeck. In later transports the figures have been higher. The majority suffer from scabies, but so far there have been no cases of typhus.

"Generally their physical condition is worse than that of previous refugees from the Russian zone, and many still bear visible traces of maltreatment. Most of the women, it was established by the examining British medical officers, had been violated, among them a girl of 10 and another of 16.

"Most of the refugees are over fifty; many in their eighties. They include sick and cripples, although the British and Poles agreed that the sick should not be sent. There are conspicuously few young people, and it appears that they are kept in Poland to do forced labour. Cases are known where children have been forcibly separated from their parents. The refugees officially are permitted to bring with them bedding and cooking utensils as well as personal belongings, but few have bedding and fewer still their cooking utensils. This is partly due to the short notice given them to leave—it has been established that ten minutes was allowed in some cases; in others no notice was given, but the house simply turned over to a new Polish settler. Also a fair amount of their luggage, especially their personal belongings, has been stolen by Poles, mainly on the journey to Stettin.

"Matters have slightly improved since a British medical team arrived in Stettin to supervise the train arrangements. Food is now likely to get better; the danger of epidemics is being lessened by the use of D.D.T. powder sent from the British zone; and the indiscriminate sending of the sick and of unaccompanied children is likely to be stopped. But so far nothing is being done to supervise the treatment of refugees on the first stage of their journey from their homes to Stettin.

"Altogether one and a half million refugees are expected to arrive in the course of the next few months, 1,500 a day by train, another 1,000 by boat. The figure is, however, likely to be nearer the two million mark . . ."

2,000,000. That's one of the troubles: we stare stupidly at the ciphers, and forget the bodies and the souls. I don't know what the position is at the moment. Shortly after the above article appeared the British issued an official protest, not of course against the expulsions, but against "the conditions of movement." They also complained "that the Polish authorities are sending an unduly high proportion of the very old, sick, and weak, and that it thus appears that there is being transferred not, as agreed at Potsdam, the whole German minority, but the less useful part of it." You can ponder over the word "useful" for quite a while. As to the protest, perhaps the Poles have attended to it and perhaps not.

*　　*　　*　　*

You have read the quotations. And now ask yourselves, is this justice—I say justice, not vengeance: is it kindness and mercy : is it a recognition of the rights of every human being : is it, in a word, respect for personality ? Will it show, by force of example, what western values mean ? Or will it sink still more deeply into these German minds the wound of fascism, so that greater and greater numbers must believe—the parents of dying children, the children of lost parents, the whole sad company of wanderers and all who watched their sufferings or heard of them from others—that brutality is the norm of human behaviour, and that when Hitler indicted the hypocrisy of democrats he was right? Will it lead to peace, or to wars of vengeance? Is it preparing the way for liberal democracy, or for ruthless totalitarianism?

IV

Perhaps even worse is the other decree of the Potsdam dictators, the spoliation and economic enslavement of Germany. It is worse than the expulsions, because, though the memory of them will be poisonous, they themselves will cease. It is worse than the annexations, because even a truncated Reich might with infinite difficulty, in the absence of positive impediments, have achieved a limited prosperity. But Potsdam was determined— in the name of security but who knows with what an intermixture of greed and vengeance ?—that nothing of the kind should be even conceivable. The idea was, in Mr. Churchill's words "to render all offensive action by Germany utterly impossible for generations to come". The thing simply cannot be done, as we have seen, and even Mr. Churchill was modest enough to speak of generations and not of eternity. But in the pauperising of Germany for decades : in the intensifying of a frustration which is the seed-bed of illiberalism : in teaching once again that might is right and right an illusion : and in adding yet a further motive to the longing for revenge—the effect must be, unless Potsdam is revised and revised speedily, to make it quite impossible to transform the German mood, and absolutely certain that when these restrictions go, as sooner or later go they will, the Germans of that generation will be the sort of people who, on their own account or by intriguing with one country against another, will use their recovered power for evil ends. The mere trifle that an "economic slum" in the heart of Europe must make nonsense of European recovery—Rotterdam is already stagnating for lack of German trade—may be mentioned by the way.

When I speak of spoliation and economic enslavement I do not mean the stealing of other people's goods as "war booty", in which the Russians particularly specialize, nor what is called "living [after victory] off the land." These, it is true, are un-amiable procedures. But I mean something less naïvely barbaric : I mean the deliberate and cold-blooded decision to strip from Germany a great part not of her income but of her productive resources, to keep her so denuded in perpetuity, and to maintain "in Germany living standards not exceeding the average of the standards of living of European countries, excluding Great Britain and the U.S.S.R." This is not, essentially, a question of reparations. There is a strong case in justice for the reparations that are a synonym for restitution ; though wisdom, and a morality more fundamental than justice of the arithmetical kind, demand that even the most grossly outraged countries, such as Poland and Russia, should forego the unfulfilled balance of their claims directly they are once again on the high road to prosperity. The aim should be, at that stage, to increase the well-being of all countries without discrimination. But if this point of view is considered Utopian, since Utopia now means not an ideal you strive for but something crazy which no sane man would even contemplate (sane signifying, in this connection, "hard-boiled"), it remains true that reparations might be obtained to the last farthing, if indeed that could ever be possible after the havoc the Nazis have wrought, by a method which would still permit an ultimate German recovery. You might refrain from destroying or removing the factories, the machines, the productive resources of the enemy : you might leave the sources of wealth intact : and you might require that an annual percentage of the wealth produced, as high as you like and for as long as you like, should be handed over in restitution. The argument against this course is so unconvincing that its honesty must be suspect. We tried that sort of thing last time, people say, and it failed : the reparations bill, at first gargantuan, became a pygmy, and finally disappeared. So it did ; but it disappeared because "we" acquiesced in, or willed, its disappearance. Circumstances changed ; German recovery became at first primarily an American and then a world interest, and as reparations interfered with it they had to go. Is it suggested that, with Germany in utter ruin and completely at the mercy of her victors, we should lack the power to exact a yearly toll of reparations? We may lack the will; but if we indeed contemplate that possibility, it is because we are already wondering whether the long-term pauperisation of Germany, which we seek to ensure once and for all by destroying the sources of her wealth, will turn out to be really wise. The moral would be, one might think, to pause before the *fait accompli*.

Equally unconvincing is the argument from security. Any but light industry, it is said, and a good deal of that, is so much war potential: a country with great plant for steel and chemicals and electricity can at a moment's notice wage aggressive war. It may be boilers in February: how do we know it won't be tanks in March? This is sheer nonsense. War potential may be more important than a stock of weapons once aggression has been launched; but how can it be launched at all without at least some accumulation, and a very considerable one at that? Only one thing is essential for security: and that is a complete ban on certain industrial end-products, namely armaments of every kind. Is it seriously suggested for a single moment that these products could be manufactured under Allied eyes or with Allied occupation, and that, if they were, even the merest fraction of the essential armament could be stored and accumulated? The easiest system of inspection would stop anything of the kind in five minutes. We, or one or other of us, may of course lack the will, just as Russia lacked it after the last war, when she helped the German General Staff to reorganise, and ourselves, when we connived at the manufacture of weapons for use against the Left: but, if so, we shall equally lack the will to prevent the Germans from rebuilding their factories and re-establishing their economy. If security cannot be got by inspection, it cannot be got by destruction.

We must face the fact that neither restitution nor security—security against German aggression—was the primary aim of the Potsdam decision, with German helotry as just a necessary consequence: it was the helotry itself that was desired, restitution and security being no more than by the way. It is interesting to speculate on the motives of these three men, who in a few hours, and during the intervals between great banquets, determined the future, but not, I am afraid, as they may have intended, for generations. "Russia's" mind, by which I mean Mr. Stalin's, is perhaps the easiest to read. To that vast territory, with its almost inexhaustible resources, European recovery must appear comparatively unimportant if material self-interest and crude economics are to be the criterion. What is vital, on the other hand, is that Europe should not be used as an arsenal and *glacis* for attacks on Russia. Mr. Stalin, I hazard, had a vision of tanks and artillery, built in a recovered Germany with Anglo-American encouragement or by Anglo-American order, advancing over the eastern plains for a capitalist onslaught on the Soviet West. He was determined to prevent it; and he could prevent it best, he thought, by assuring that the very minimum should be left in Germany which could ever be used for this purpose. It was not the enemy, but his Allies, that he feared. Moreover, there would be by-products, and very attractive ones, in the working of the plan. Spoliation would give him means for his own reconstruction without any tedious waiting—here reparations came in; and a helot Germany could be more easily incorporated, formally or informally, in the Soviet Union, and, when once in his grip, could safely be reindustrialised as he might desire. The preliminary moves in this game are being played, indeed, before our very eyes.

"America's" motive, by which I mean Mr. Roosevelt's, was far simpler, and I excuse myself from discussing it. As to Mr. Churchill, the explanation is to be found, if I guess aright, in the weaknesses which often accompany the kind of strength, so buoyant and romantic, that saved our country. One thing at a time for him: for years, the Nazi menace; from '39 to '45, victory; at Potsdam, Allied unity; now, the threat of communism. He must have been at a singular disadvantage, too, in the jovial atmosphere of the Potsdam compound. He is a warm-hearted romantic, and Mr. Stalin what is called a cold realist; and if a clash between two such men impended, it would always be the romantic who, in the flush of victory and for the sake of good-fellowship, would give way. And another psychological factor must be borne in mind. Mr. Churchill, in spite of frequent appearances to the contrary, is a man of deep liberal instincts; there is no reason to doubt his sincerity when he said, in 1940, that on the morrow of victory we would give the Germans—he emphasised the Germans—food, freedom and peace, nor again when only the other day, at Fulton, he characterised as "wrongful" and "grievous" the very decisions which he himself had made, or connived at, only a year before. But, in obsessional types, a transformation takes place under the pressure of events and the domination of a leading idea; and it took place in Mr. Churchill. Just as there was at first a scrupulous selection of military objectives, then saturation bombing, and finally Hiroshima, so as revelation succeeded revelation of Nazi bestialities Mr. Churchill's thoughts were coloured, to the exclusion of everything else, by the wickedness of "the enemy"; and when at Potsdam the choice was between remembering his liberal principles and succumbing to the idea that "the Germans" were not worth bothering about, his whole mental atmosphere impelled him to succumb.

Whatever may have been the motives, the decision was taken. Is the meaning of this counter-revolution, for that is what we are enforcing, even now understood? We have railed for decades against systems and practices that restrict production: we have dreamed of an age of plenty: and now we say to seventy million people, who are among the most industrious in Europe, "You shall produce, not for a few years but for generations, only a fraction of the wealth you are capable of producing". And when the aim should be to level up and not to level down, we say to these same seventy million "You and your children and your children's children shall live at a fixed level of poverty that we, in our wisdom, have statistically determined". Each dictate, of course, implies the other. In the matter of food Germany was never self-supporting, even at the climax of her efforts. We now lop off her richest food-producing territories: we crowd into the trunk millions from East Prussia, from Silesia, from the Sudetenland, and from anywhere else where a single German can be found: and we prevent a swollen population in a smaller and poorer Reich from producing the goods with which, in a sane economy, she might pay for the food and other imports essential for a decent standard of living.

This then was Potsdam. Just how hard and grey the general existence would be, until changed circumstances upset the whole arrangement, would depend on the exact figure at which permissible production would be fixed—on the number of factories and the amount of plant which the Allies, after their interim spoliations, would finally decide to remove or destroy. They wrangled about this for months; and it must be quickly acknowledged that, the Potsdam decision once taken, our statesmen made every effort, as might have been expected if my analysis of motives is correct, to interpret it, not liberally, for a liberal interpretation could never be possible, but with some regard for reason and humanity.

The result of these prolonged deliberations was at last announced, nearly two months late, in the "Plan for Reparations and the level of post-war German economy" of March 28th 1946. This plan is some sort of compromise between Russian severity and British qualms. I shall not describe it, for this is an essay about morals, not an economic treatise: I shall content myself with quoting a single sentence from *The Economist's* devastating analysis. "One is bound to reach the conclusion" wrote that journal on April 6th "that what is planned for Germany is a standard of living far below the average European standard and Germany's own standard of the Great Depression [1929-1933]." And I will go on to quote a moderately worded statement of what the Great Depression meant in Germany. It was written by my dear friend Hans Vogel, the socialist leader, who died here in exile soon after the end of the war:

"I should like to add a few words on the economic position in July 1932 and the following months. The situation in the labour market was disastrous. The decreasing purchasing power of people of all professions had caused a big slump in consumption goods. The application of 'rationalisation' (economy in factories) resulted in a sharp decrease in the number of occupied workers. The number of fully unemployed people rose to six millions. Out of all the workers organised in Trade Unions only one-quarter was fully employed at the end of 1931; more than one-quarter did part-time work, and nearly 50 per cent. were unemployed. At the same time nominal wages were steadily lowered and the contributions to social insurance rose, while the progressive social reforms, achieved by the workers at times of prosperity and with the aid of their political influence and their Trade Unions, were being abolished . . .

"Almost all sections of the population were affected by the crisis. The bulk of the petty and medium officials received, in many cases, lower salaries than the workers. One reduction of salary followed another at very short intervals. The small shop-keepers, idle behind empty counters, formed a part of the vast army of unemployed people, and this part was not counted in statistics and was socially neglected. They looked with envy at the salaries of officials and employees, at the wages of the workers, and even at the dole of the unemployed. The small and moderately prosperous peasants rightly complained of the low prices of the goods they produced and the high prices of the articles needed for their life and work. They were overburdened by debts and did not know what to do. In addition, there was a big 'professional proletariat'—doctors without patients, lawyers without clients, etc. Many students came from the impoverished middle-class. There were too many intellectuals, who were ill-paid when they finished their studies and began to earn their living. In the streets and the meeting-halls, in newspapers and in Parliament, the National Socialists could be heard crying that the Republic and Democracy, the 'System' and 'Marxism', 'Jewish finance' and the 'big Jewish stores' were solely responsible for this need and misery. And the Capitalists, the big industrialists, bankers, estate owners and those officers who had been dismissed after the last world war and had become something like mercenaries in the meantime, were among those who shouted most fiercely. These debased gentlemen (who included some workers—especially the unemployed ones) did not sing the Internationale, but marched singing the Horst Wessel song behind flags with crooked crosses. The slogan was not revolution, but counter-revolution.''

That is the sort of Germany that we are now "planning" for 1949.

A couple of figures may be added. In the spring elections of 1928 Hitler, for all his years of propaganda, won only twelve seats in the Reichstag out of a total of about six hundred. In July 1932 he won two hundred and thirty. 1928 was before the Depression: in July 1932 things were as Vogel describes.

*　　*　　*　　*

But what I want to emphasise again is the psychological effect of all this *now* on German minds. Restriction, frustration, the sense of being shackled, the certainty that whatever you do and however hard you work you and your children can never get beyond a point that has been fixed for you by others—these are the enemies of the liberal outlook. Is it conceivable that a country hemmed in like this can seek peace, love freedom, and respect itself and others? Which makes people saner, hope or despair? Is a gnawing sense of grievance the best recipe for mental health, or the conviction that justice has been done to you, and that you should therefore do it to your neighbour? In a word, will Potsdam strengthen western values in Germany, or still further weaken them?

V

For this policy of economic enslavement, as for the annexation of territories and expulsion of populations, we and our Allies are jointly responsible: but we have done things in the British zone for which the responsibility is solely ours. On the morrow of victory we shut ourselves off, by deliberate decree, from all intercourse with the conquered people; and now, in the spring of 1946, we are starving them.

I have before me the text of Field-marshal Viscount Montgomery's broadcast to the Germans on June 10th 1945, explaining why every soldier had been ordered "to keep clear of German man, woman and child unless you meet them in the course of duty". It is an amazing document. Its patent falsehoods are not, perhaps, of much importance. The statements that "your leaders" started the war of 1914, whereas in fact its roots lie deep in international and economic history: or that in the Treaty of Versailles "your leaders" admitted that Germany was responsible for the war and later on repudiated the war guilt paragraph, whereas they signed this paragraph in protest and under duress, and one has only to read the *Encyclopædia Britannica* to see what responsible British opinion subsequently thought about it: or that "when your leaders once more wantonly unleashed this war you applauded them", whereas observer after observer then in Germany, from William Shirer downwards, has testified in print to the precise opposite—such statements can no doubt be dismissed as mere hangovers from war-time propaganda. But what is so horrifying in this document is its personalising of almost meaningless abstractions —"you", "Germany", "the Germans"—and its consequent depersonalising of actual men and women. What Montgomery is saying is that the mythical, the non-existent "you", "your nation", is "guilty" of the whole cycle of iniquity—of starting both wars, 1914 and 1939, of shooting and ruining and starving, of laughing at carnage and outrage—and that this mythical "you" must be made to realise "its" guilt by being treated as a pariah: whereupon, hey presto, the mythical "you" is identified with the real yous—with every actual, concrete, living man and woman —and every one of the real yous must be treated as a pariah. "You" raped Belgium in 1914: so women now twenty did so, and should be boycotted. "You" sent men to Buchenwald: so the inmates of Buchenwald did so, and should be boycotted. "You" were jubilant, "you" celebrated and laughed—these are Montgomery's words: so mothers of the killed and maimed and missing did so, and should be boycotted. Even the little children are "you": Montgomery instructs his hearers "to read this to your children if they are old enough, and see that they understand it. Explain to them why English soldiers do not pay any attention to them."

This horrible vice of personalising a race or nation and depersonalising the individuals that make it up is of course nothing new. The Jews have suffered particularly from it. "The Jews", you hear, are this or that—capitalists or communists, money-lenders or philanthropists, cosmopolitans or nationalists, according to taste. But if there were a hundred Jews in the world, and ninety-nine of them were capitalists, it would still be untrue, and totally untrue, that "the Jews" were capitalists: ninety-nine particular Jews would be capitalists and one particular Jew not. So with "the Germans" and "the French" and "the English" and everyone else. No, this sort of thing is nothing new. What is new in the present instance is that this shoddy emotional vulgarism was officially adopted by a Government no longer at war, and made the basis, in its extreme form, of actual policy. Even this, however, was not entirely new. Hitler, before 1939 and of course with far greater brutality, had provided a precedent.

But it must not be thought that non-fraternisation was objectionable merely because every German, just for being a German, came under the ban, no distinction being drawn between the obviously "innocent" and the obviously or even supposedly "guilty", between men like Marshal Goering and men like Pastor Grüber, between Buchenwald torturers and helpless children. The objection is far more fundamental than that; the objection is to the whole policy of non-fraternisation as such, irrespective of the individuals to whom it may be applied. People said everything about it at the time except the one thing that mattered. Would it produce the desired result? Was it fair to our soldiers? How long should it be maintained?—these were the questions that everyone was asking. No one of standing, so far as I can recall, neither churchman nor humanitarian nor socialist, said quite plainly that, whatever the answers to these particular questions might be, non-fraternisation, which means "not treating a man as a brother", was just simply wicked. "We are a Christian people" said Montgomery, when "explaining" this policy to the Germans. But what he really meant, as the context shows, was this: "Sometime or other we shall behave like Christians, when and if, but only when and if, you show us that you have given up your unchristian Nazism." That seems to me, as a Jew who believes in Christian ethics, a somewhat heretical application of Christ's teaching: and fifty bishops will not make me, who can read the New Testament as well as they, think otherwise.

It was for fraternity, for human brotherhood that we had, in the last analysis, been fighting. What does human brotherhood mean? It means a free communication, in spiritual equality, between man and man: a contact not so much demanded by, as identical with, sympathy: a relationship mediated by speech, and issuing both from, and in, mutual assistance. That the nature of man demands this brotherhood is the faith, surely, that for six long years of unspeakable agony we had been defending: we wanted a world where its practice would be possible, not one in which, as Hitler dreamed, some men, no longer really men at all, would be acted on by others. If we really understand fraternity, we must understand also that what the other man may have done is irrelevant, or relevant only in the sense that fraternity with him is something we shall find it harder, and therefore more imperative, to achieve. Only saints can be at one, as if by nature, with those who have wronged them or whom they know to have wronged others; and only a pharisee would criticise a man for feeling cold to someone who has ruined his life or brought disaster on millions. But precisely because that barrier which divides even lovers is strongest between a wrongdoer and one who has been wronged or seen others wronged, a special effort must be made in just that case to overcome it; and while repentance by the wrongdoer may be the first step to reconciliation, a kind of honour requires that forgiveness, even for wrongs committed against others, should take the initiative. I would add that I use the words

115

"repentance" and "forgiveness" not in their exact senses but, by way of analogy, to suggest what language is incapable of expressing: for while we can restore to men we can repent only to God, and while men can sympathise (or wish well) only God can forgive. I would add, also, that such words as "wrongdoers" and "the wronged" are employed only in an attempt to make my argument clear. A wise man would avoid them: he would obey the injunction "Judge not, that ye be not judged", and remember that if everybody had his deserts no one would escape whipping.

This question of fraternising with the really "guilty" (and a great many Germans are neither more nor less "guilty" than a great many Englishmen) might perhaps be summed up by saying that to be at one, or rather to endeavour to be at one, with a man we judge bad is more important than to be at one with a man we judge good; and that, detesting murder, it is precisely with the murderer that we must shake hands, not only physically but in the spirit. Good must be reinforced at the point where evil is strongest.

The horror of non-fraternisation was that having fought the war for human brotherhood we made a studied policy of outraging it. We did not allow the individual to decide, as his moral strength or weakness might dictate: we said, quite deliberately, "you will be punished if you treat a single one of these people as a brother". We dried up, or attempted to dry up, the springs of human sympathy; and speech, which distinguishes men from the beasts, and guarantees the existence, as it marked the birth, of a spiritual society, was denied. "You have often wondered" said Montgomery "why our soldiers do not pay any attention when you wave to them or bid them 'Good morning' in the street, and why they do not play with your children. Our soldiers are acting in accordance with orders." They were orders as psychologically stupid as they were morally repugnant. The idea was to bring home to "the Germans", by a display of cold contempt, a sense of their overwhelming guilt. But wasn't it against all wisdom and experience to imagine that even those, and they were many, who might reasonably feel responsible for some at least of the outrages attributed to them, would respond as apparently they were expected to respond to this treatment? Does a man's character commonly improve when his nose is rubbed in the dirt? Does contempt soften people, or harden them?

The ban, of course, could not last, and was eventually discontinued amid a spate of ribaldries. Before the subject is left, two stories are worth recalling. The first is certainly untrue, but its invention shows, in that folk way which is more effective than pages of exposition, what an outrage on human relationships non-fraternisation was. The men were told, it is said, that they could sleep with German girls with impunity, provided they did not speak to them before, during, or after the intercourse. The other story is typical, I have no doubt, of thousands. An American column was marching down the street of a German village. On the pavement was a little boy asking for chocolate; to give it would have been to fraternise, so everyone looked grimly ahead. But a few yards further on one of the soldiers ran out of the ranks, threw back a bit of chocolate, ran back to his place, turned to the man on his right, and said with a glare "So what?" Human decency, stronger than all the generals in the world, had broken through.

VI

We non-fraternised with the Germans in the summer of 1945 : we are starving them in the spring of 1946. And we are starving them, not deliberately in the sense that we definitely want them to die, but wilfully in the sense that we prefer their death to our own inconvenience : by which I mean that we prefer utter misery for them, with death as an often inevitable consequence, to any serious reduction in our own relatively very high standard of living, or even to the possibility that at some future date such a reduction might have to be effected. The only qualification we admit is that their misery must stop short at the point below which any semblance of orderly administration would become impossible.

This is our real policy ; but its true nature is largely concealed by the three propositions with which the Government defends its world food policy as a whole. They are as follows : (1) We have all along been making every possible sacrifice for the relief of distress wherever it may occur. (2) In the general share-out our first duty is to fight for the interests of our Empire (which means chiefly India) and our Allies, towards whom we have a special responsibility. (3) The Germans properly come at the end of the queue.

1

The first proposition, I reply, is patently untrue.

What are the facts? I am sorry to have to trouble the reader with details about calories, but the position simply will not be understood unless I do.

(a) "A diet containing an average of about 2,650* calories a day . . ." says the report of the Emergency Economic Committee for Europe, issued on February 6th 1946, "has been recommended by the Unrra Food Committee as the amount of food sufficient to maintain full health and efficiency in a population with a normal distribution according to sex, age and occupation. . . . An average diet of around 2,000 calories has been generally recognised . . . as a minimum level below which there would be marked effects on ability to work and danger of . . . disease . . . . These effects become progressively more serious as the diet is reduced down to and below 1,500 calories and the period of low diet is prolonged."

(b) During the whole period since victory our own average daily calories have never fallen below 2,850†. This figure has been repeatedly given in the House of Commons, and I was informed a very short time ago to this effect by the Ministry of Food.

(c) During 1945 (the last period for which comparative official figures are available) our average daily consumption was only about 10 per cent. a head less than that in the most favoured country of all, the United States of America ; and in April this year we were officially stated to be consuming, on the average, only 5 per cent. less than we ourselves consumed before the war.

(d) Sir Wilson Jameson, Chief Medical Officer to the Ministry of Health, told a Press conference on November 16th 1945 that

---

* Calories are units of heat: in nutrition, so many calories mean so many units that "stoke up" the body. The following point should be noted. The calories cited in official figures may be calories of food at the retail level—in the shops—or of food in actual consumption. As there is a wastage in the shops and in the house, a small deduction must be made from the first figure to arrive at the second—about 10%. Official and semi-official figures rarely state whether they refer to the retail or the consumption level, and in any event the difference is too small to affect any argument that follows to the slightest degree. In general, it may be supposed that desirable levels of diet refer to consumption, and figures of actual daily intake usually, but not always, to food in the shops.

† But see footnote above.

there was no evidence whatever of any weakening of the physical health of the people of this country, which had been "astonishingly good."

(e) The latest annual Summary Report of the Ministry of Health (for the year ended March 31st 1945) stated that death-rates among mothers in childbirth, babies in their first month of life, and children of all ages up to five were the lowest ever recorded in England and Wales, in war or in peace ; so were the death-rates for tuberculosis, diphtheria and typhoid fever, and the standardised death-rates for both men and women.

(f) The Combined Food Board reported in November 1945 that while the fats and vitamin A in our diet were down by 13 and 10 per cent. respectively in comparison with pre-war figures, there was an increase in proteins of 11 per cent., in calcium of 49 per cent., in iron of 15 per cent. and in vitamin C of 20 per cent., carbohydrates remaining the same : and although average figures conceal the extent to which these increases have gone to the priority classes, Dr. Magee, in a Milroy Lecture before the Royal College of Physicians on March 14th 1946, concluded that "the general state of nutrition of the population as a whole has been up to, or above, pre-war standards".

Now for the other side of the picture :

(a) Before November 12th 1945 ration scales for normal consumers in the British zone of Germany had differed in different regions, ranging from a minimum of 1,050 calories to a maximum of 1,591. On November 12th a uniform scale was established of 1,550 calories, and this remained in force till March 4th of the present year. In the period between victory and March 4th, therefore, there had been, on paper, actual starvation in certain regions, as well as varying degrees of malnutrition throughout the zone. But the situations on paper and in fact were not identical. What is called "the farm population" was adequately and sometimes more than adequately fed, as farm populations everywhere almost invariably are : and even in the small and large towns some people were able to supplement the ration from reserves of their own or by getting extras from friends in the country. Nevertheless the evidence of misery on an appalling scale—I am speaking now of the period before March 4th, and of the ordinary population, not of refugees from the East—is overwhelming. I have given a good deal of it elsewhere* : I will give only a fraction of it here.

* Leaving Them to Their Fate, Gollancz, 1946.

Charles Bray, *Daily Herald* Berlin correspondent, wrote on August 30th 1945 that the ration in that city, which was then officially, on the average, 1,500, was in fact just enough to keep a man alive if he remained in bed and did not exert himself at all ; and that during the month July 12th to August 11th there were 609 births and 2,700 deaths, the total population (British area) being 547,000. The effect of the food situation, wrote the *Times* correspondent from Herford on September 6th, was reflected in the rate of mortality among babies in one British-controlled borough of the capital, which for the period from May 6th to August 13th totalled 594, compared with 60 for the corresponding period of 1944. "Misery," wrote *The Observer's* correspondent from Cologne on September 8th, "is bending down their heads and wiping the last faint smile off their faces. Their nerves are already breaking down. Signs of demoralisation leap to one's eyes." During that month, according to Dr. George Stuart, head of the Medical Information Branch of Unrra, typhoid fever had reached 30 times its normal incidence in Germany. Miss Ellen Wilkinson, on her return to this country on October 7th after a visit to Germany, made no attempt to conceal the position: "There is no doubt" she said "that quite a number of children will die before the winter ends because food cannot be got off to them. That is principally in Berlin, which is the central problem." This, it will be remembered, was about the date when the cut in fats was being restored in this country, and when Dr. Edith Summerskill, Parliamentary Secretary to the Ministry of Food, was giving it as her opinion (October 17th) that the time had come when Britain must not only restore rations but must try to increase them.

(b) A drastic cut in German rations was announced on February 27th this year, to come into operation on March 4th. They were to go down to 1,014 for normal consumers (a category which includes most women other than expectant and nursing mothers and nursing staffs in hospitals and institutions, and, as Mr. Hynd subsequently told the House, numbers some ten million persons) with corresponding reductions for other categories. This was a trifle below the figure that had ruled in some regions before November 12th. But the position was different now. Owing to the exhaustion of reserves, there would be far less likelihood of supplementing this ration than had been the case some months before.

"It would be hard to exaggerate" wrote the *Manchester Guardian* correspondent from Herford "the seriousness of the food situation in the zone. A diet of 1,000 calories means trying to live on about two slices of bread with, perhaps, a smear of margarine, a spoonful of porridge, and two not very large potatoes. Bread, potatoes and porridge make up four-fifths of the average German's present diet, and the amount of other food he gets is very little . . . Cuts in the ration for expectant mothers are tragic. December figures (the latest available) show infant mortality in the British zone of about one hundred and fifty per thousand, which means that between three and four babies are dying here for every infant who dies in England. . . . These are the figures on existing rations, but they foreshadow clearly enough the probable effects of severe cuts in food."

It was at this time that the general principles of the Government's food policy, to which I referred at the beginning of this section, were announced. "The British Government" wrote *The Manchester Guardian* "has been considering whether any grain supplies could go to Germany *without prejudicing the food standard in Britain* [my emphasis] and other countries. At present the Government's view is that there are no such resources which can be diverted. In addition to our own big food problem, we have obligations to India and other lands in which we are particularly interested. Then there are the liberated territories of Europe calling for help. These and other factors, it is felt, take precedence over Germany's needs. Germany must be looked upon as coming at the end of the world's food queue."
"At the end of the queue" became a catchword, repeated in speech after speech and newspaper after newspaper. But *The Daily Express*, which has a flair for headlines, was more original. It preferred the formula "Must Be Left to Their Fate."

At about the same time there was an article in *The Manchester Guardian* from its Special Correspondent in the Ruhr. I am going to quote the major part of it:

"Words like 'famine' and 'hunger' sound much more dramatic as words than is the reality of their appearance in homes and streets. Famine does not sweep a countryside like war—it creeps slowly through great cities and is realised only gradually as small stores of food dwindle and each week there is less and less to replace what has been eaten. Hunger is a grey thing and it kills drearily, masking its killing in a hundred ways. Famine must go on for months before this visible horror of starvation comes; there is a swelling tide of illness and death among people who do not get enough to eat.

" There is hunger in the Ruhr today, but it is still undramatic and to be seen indirectly in such things as infant mortality and dwindling output from the mines. There has not yet been time for the food cuts of March 4 to be reflected in statistics, but the Ruhr was beginning to be hungry before these cuts were imposed. In Dortmund in February, out of 257 children born, 46 died, which is rather more than four times as many infant deaths as the English average rate would show. In Cologne the infant death-rate rose from 164 per 1,000 in January to 170 in February. These figures are enough to show a statistical background of hunger and bad living conditions against which the drastic recent food cuts must be seen.

" A week spent visiting the great industrial cities of Dortmund, Essen, and Dusseldorf coalmining districts around Bochum and Unna, and small towns on the fringes of the Ruhr, like Iserlohn and Ludenscheid, has enabled one to form a fairly clear impression of actual conditions now in this all-important area of the British zone. The big towns and mining districts are incomparably worse off than the fringe towns which have access to the countryside. I visited a mining family yesterday near Unna and found them at a meal. There was no food whatever on the table for five people but a few slices of bread, about an ounce of margarine among the five of them, and cups of milkless ersatz coffee.

" The father, who was ill, had a cup of thin gruel made with milk which was allowed him because of his illness. He got a quarter of a litre of milk a day, and this was the only milk in the house. They said that they got enough bread to give them about two slices apiece a day, and they had a little meat once a week. They had enough dried beans to make a thin soup most days, and the very small quantity of oatmeal or ryemeal that the reduced ration now allows them could also be used in soup. Occasionally they got a salted herring. They had no potatoes at all, and it was this complete lack of potatoes and extreme shortage of bread that they really felt.

" Apart from oddments which do not amount to much, basically these people are living on about two slices of bread a day and a cup of bean soup. They are not exceptional, for I questioned several other miners at random in the district and all had much the same story to tell. The working miners get a canteen meal at the mine of soup, three thinnish slices of bread, and—if they are underground workers—one slice of sausage. They are not supposed to take any of this food home, but it is quite obvious that married men do take home what they can spare to give to their wives. . . .

" This is the picture of life in the Ruhr today, of hunger that is intensely real, although not yet dramatic, and of a situation that is intensely dangerous both politically and economically. The small increase in meat, fish and sugar that has been promised for next month will do little to improve things, for the desperate shortage is in bread, grains, and potatoes. Between the Ruhr and complete economic collapse is the slender barrier of two slices of bread a day."

Mr. Gerald Barry, editor of *The News Chronicle* (one of the newspapers that have given a lead for decency since the beginning of this business) wrote on March 11th after completing a visit to Germany:

" But for the German who has nothing to fall back on and is not in one of the privileged categories, the actual daily ration is now as low as the prisoners of Belsen received in the worst days. On paper the ration is 1,000 calories. Translate this into bread and butter. It means $2\frac{1}{2}$ rounds of bread a day, $1\frac{1}{4}$ oz. of flour for cooking, $\frac{1}{2}$ oz. of fat, a literal mouthful of meat, about a tablespoonful of sugar, half a cupful of skim-milk—and three mythical potatoes. *The potatoes do not exist.* The only Germans who are getting potatoes on the ration today are the two classes of heavy mineworkers at their canteen meals—if they are lucky. As this potato ration, which exists only on paper, represents 185 calories out of a total 1,000 the actual calorie ration of the ordinary German in the British zone today is 815. Set out on a table, this ration is barely sufficient for one good breakfast—and nothing more for the day."

The Daily Express, however, felt able to publish, on March 25th, " the conclusions from answers given to investigators for the Daily Express Centre of Public Opinion by a representative cross section of the public." " Public opinion," they found, was almost equally divided on the question whether or not we get enough to eat. 55 per cent. were dissatisfied with the way in which the Government was handling the food situation. The dissatisfied "condemned the policy of feeding Germans while Britain's rations were so meagre." I wrote a letter to the journal giving the salient facts. It was not published.

(c) In case you should want something official, Sir Jack Drummond, Scientific Adviser to the Ministry of Food, said on March 27th 1946 that at the level of 1,000 calories "one can without any hesitation speak of starvation".

* * * *

In the light of this evidence—about our own standard of living on the one hand, and the German on the other—have we in fact, I ask, "all along been doing everything possible"? I wish this were something that reasonable people might argue about, something about which there might be legitimate differences of opinion. That, unhappily, is not the case. We must charge ourselves, without any possibility of rebuttal, with a degree of selfishness of which we shall live to be most bitterly ashamed. We have been less selfish, certainly, than most or perhaps any, and far less selfish than some : but it would be a queer kind of patriotism that sought in such a plea the grant of absolution.

By "we" I mean, of course, we as a nation, we in our national policy. I do not mean that, as the *Daily Express* "Centre of Public Opinion" might lead you to expect, Britain, or 55 per cent of it, is one solid mass of individual selfishness. That is just untrue : I have any amount of evidence to the contrary. I could fill a volume with the letters that came in when the "Save Europe Now" organisation was trying to rouse this same "public opinion" last autumn. One man wrote from a hospital where he had been lying sick for two years as a result of his treatment by the Nazis. "I need food to make me well," he said, "but I would willingly lie here for another two years if by doing so I could save a single child, German or otherwise, from suffering." Another letter came from a miner, who wrote on behalf of forty other miners in the same village. "Each of us is willing," he wrote, "to take an undernourished child from Europe into our homes, if they can be brought here, and to share our rations with them, if we have to. We don't mind if they are German." That miner was speaking for Britain and for socialism. Mr. Will Lawther, the miners' leader, was not, when he gave a display quite recently of that detestable sentimentality which masquerades as "toughness." British miners, he said, had been generous to their foreign comrades, but not a penny piece would they give to German miners in their need. He may or may not have forgotten that German miners helped British miners in the strike of '26.

No, I am not accusing the public. On the contrary, if it were not impertinent I should praise them warmly for grumbling far less than might have been expected in the circumstances. For they were simply not allowed to know until this spring what the position actually was : they were so deafened by talk about their personal inconveniences that, even if now and again a bit of real information did get through the barrage, few of them could have any effective realisation of what life was meaning for so many, or any vivid sense of contrast between the agony of others and their own more favourable situation. And to say "more favourable" is to put the position with extreme moderation. Discomfort and monotony, of course, there have been ; luxuries have been lacking ; queuing has been a bore. For some special classes, such as single people living alone on small means, life has been particularly drab and difficult. But in the name of all decency or sense of proportion what are things like these in comparison with the awful grey misery, day after day, of real hunger and starvation, until in the end death comes in its most hideous form?

It is the Press I accuse, or the baser part of it : and I shall have something to say about that presently. But above all I accuse the Government, which in some other respects has deserved so well of the country. Whether because it really thinks that way, or because it has been afraid to ask of our people what the overwhelming majority of them, in their fundamental generosity, would have been willing and happy to give if bravely led and adequately informed, it has made us all its accomplices in a national policy which is quite unworthy of what Mr. Churchill called, in a speech I shall quote later, " our customs and our nature."

Forget all about Germany. Cut out that complication altogether. Remember only, if you will, that during the whole of this period, when our own calories were being maintained at 2,850, millions in Europe—allies, ex-enemies, and people like the Italians who were half one and half the other—were in varying degrees of wretchedness, from horrible malnutrition to actual starvation. I will give only one example, that of Vienna, and I choose it because while Unrra was giving some assistance elsewhere it was barred until recently from Austria. Now listen. Sir George Franckenstein, who had been Austrian Minister in London from 1920 to 1938, wrote an article early this year after his return from a visit to that country. " I visited the home for old people at Linz, with 3,500 inmates " he said " of whom at present, only 10 per cent are in normal health. In its gigantic kitchen I tasted the daily meal of peas. The taste and smell of the food sickened me. It was unsalted, owing to shortage of salt. . . . I asked a poor woman whose limbs were completely paralysed if she had any wish as to food ; with infinite difficulty she moved her lips, uttering pathetically only the one magic word ' Atropin ' (the medicament which would give her so much relief but is completely lacking). Both for the old people and the children, of whom 40,000 in Vienna alone are terribly undernourished, fats, milk, cocoa, sugar, vitamins, medicaments, clothing and shoes are sorely needed." There is no question here of "innocence" or "guilt" : even crazy pharisees will remember that Austria was one of Hitler's earliest victims. As to the more recent situation in Austria, it may be judged from the fact that, according to *The Times* of March 20th, "A Viennese doctor of international reputation . . . said that nothing could be done for the aged of Vienna except to give them an injection which would cause death without pain."

The position in Europe as a whole, about which there had been a great deal of uncoordinated information for months, was revealed in February 1946 by the report of the Emergency Economic Committee for Europe, to which I have already referred. Let me put down again the figures given in its preamble : 2,650 calories as sufficient to maintain full health and efficiency, 2,000 as a minimum level below which there would be marked effects on ability to work and danger of disease, these effects becoming progressively serious as the diet is reduced down to and below 1,500 calories and the period of low diet is prolonged. The Committee found that during the following few months some 100 million people in Europe, including the non-farm populations of Austria, Germany, and Italy, would probably be receiving an average daily diet of 1,500 calories or less, and that another 40 million, including millions in France and Czechoslovakia, would probably be receiving an average of more than 1,500 but less than 2,000. Our own calories, I repeat, were 2,850. Very few people knew anything about this report, which was published in full, so far as I am aware, in only one paper, *The Manchester Guardian*. The reason for its virtual suppression is a very shameful one : that was the time of the cut in dried egg, which was better news. And the Committee, as we now know, gravely underestimated.

Leave Germany, then, out of the reckoning altogether, and still isn't it fantastic to pretend, in view of all this, that we have done everything within our power? The Government makes great play with the fact that after liberation we sent tons of food to our starving Allies, who otherwise would have been in most desperate plight. So we did. We sent them something over a million tons from the colossal reserves of 6 million that we had been building up ; and it will always be a pleasure to remember that we did far more for them than any other country in comparison with our resources. But can it be suggested that this relieved us of all further responsibility? For we stopped short, be it remembered, at the point where any significant diminution of our own comfort would be involved ; we stopped short, too, at the point where even the maintenance of that comfort at some future date might be seriously threatened. We saw to it that we retained at the end of March this year, in the ownership and control of the Ministry of Food and exclusive of all stocks on farms or held by secondary wholesalers and certain manufacturers, some four million tons of food and feeding stuffs.

You hear two arguments which are supposed to prove quite conclusively that we couldn't, and shouldn't, have been doing anything more. The first is that others (by which is chiefly meant the United States) have been in a better position to help than we have. This is unquestionably true: but I find the argument unattractive. If the good Samaritan had made a calculation like that the name of his despised and insignificant people would not have become an immortal synonym for decency. The second argument is that we owe it, alternatively to ourselves or to the world, that we should have a strong population capable of producing the maximum of wealth. That sort of argument is always a little suspect : it is what is known as "too convenient." Quite a number of things might be said about it : for instance, if it is really the world we are thinking about, and if we really want a maximum of total production, why are we despoiling Germany of her plant and factories, and undermining the health of her industrial population? That seems an odd way of getting wealth. Already, since these latest cuts, the production of Ruhr coal, on which European recovery depends, and other kinds of production in the British zone, have dropped disastrously. But in fact the whole argument, employed as it is employed, is shoddy and devoid of substance: it has no greater validity than has "charity begins at home" as a plea for selfishness. The types of heavy workers that require particularly big meals for efficiency are not statistically of great importance; their rations could even be increased, and there would still be ample margins for a net economy. How could production have been affected by the differential bread rationing which has been consistently advocated and is even yet not adopted as I write, and which would have saved a great tonnage of bread without the loss of so much as a slice a day to a single heavy worker, or, for the matter of that, to a single child or adolescent? Again, Sir Ben Smith was urged last autumn to require the surrender of a one-point coupon for every meal consumed in a luxury restaurant. He summarily refused. Was that in the interests of production? Do heavy workers eat at the Ritz? Similarly with a number of other proposals. I am not suggesting that anything should have been done which might seriously have impaired our productive ability; for when we are honestly thinking not of our own comfort or wealth but of world prosperity—and how difficult that is, since self-deception is almost impossible to avoid—the argument from production is valid enough. But when used for the purpose of maintaining our general standards unimpaired it is the merest ballyhoo.

* * * *

But at any rate, it will be said, the Government did do something this spring. Happily, yes. But on an adequate scale? With the requisite urgency? In the spirit that a proud people would have desired? I cannot think so. The story can be quickly told.

The vigorous Mr. LaGuardia's appointment as head of Unrra, synchronising with the humanitarian Mr. Hoover's visit to Europe, changed the whole situation. The imminent starvation of tens or even hundreds of millions became headline news, and could no longer be treated *piano*. Mr. Hoover called on Britain to release 500,000 tons of bread-foods which, he alleged, she was carrying, additionally to the amount of her pre-war stocks, in reserve or in the pipe-line. This tonnage, he said, must be sent to Europe immediately, for it was the nearest source of supply, and the urgency was not one of weeks but of days. Britain said she would send or divert less than half this amount, but only against a "signed and sealed" guarantee of very early replacement by America. America gave the guarantee. Britain undertook to introduce bread rationing if America would do the same. America refused, but, in addition to some other measures, cut the distribution of wheat to millers by 25 per cent. instead. The British Cabinet, reassembling after the Easter holidays, announced that it would not ration bread, but would reduce the weight of the loaf while maintaining its price, and would cut the amount of barley to be used for brewing (some 800,000 tons a year) by 15 per cent. There would be a reduction in the price of certain food-stuffs to balance the increase in the price of bread, so that there might be no alteration in the cost of living. A little later two further measures were announced: a reduction in the amount of grain, sugar and fats to be used for biscuits and confectionery (followed almost at once by an improvement in our sweets ration), and an increase in the extraction rate of wheat to 90 per cent.—which, though it involves the risk of fewer pigs and poultry later on, gives us a more nutritious loaf.

Asked if he regarded the above "cuts" as final, Sir Ben Smith is reported to have said at his Press Conference on May 2nd: "I can only go on hoping," and to have added "I would say the cuts we are making are equal to what the United States have done". So inch by inch, with a nice arithmetic of generosity and a careful balancing of one country's sacrifices against another's, the Government has yielded. Later in May Mr. Morrison flew to America, and after lengthy bargaining agreed at the last minute, not to release any wheat from our stocks or pipe-line, but to forgo 200,000 tons "due" to us between then and September, this time without a guarantee of replacement. In return, America promised to help with India and the British zone of Germany, where otherwise rations would have fallen to 500 calories—a figure which would have meant a horrible death for millions, and in a matter of weeks or even days. Bread rationing is now being discussed, and may have been introduced before this essay appears. But let us keep a sense of proportion about it, and remember, first, that we were the only European country whose bread was unrationed during the war, and secondly, that if all children, adolescents and heavy workers consumed as much as at present, and the rest of us ate only one thin slice a day less, the saving would be some 300,000 tons a year. Rationing might, indeed, involve no loss in consumption at all; the result might simply be to eliminate waste.

It need not be pointed out the measures taken by the Government this spring at once made nonsense of its previous case. If they could do what they did in April, inadequate though in my view it was, they could have done it, and far more, in the summer and autumn of last year, when there was already such appalling suffering in Europe, or in the winter, when the crisis deepened, or in February, when the cut in German rations to 1000 calories was announced. On the Government's assumption that these are really effective measures, no one can say how many thousands of lives would have been saved, or how many hundreds of thousands of men, women and children would have been spared extreme suffering, if action had been prompter. The "too late" in peace may not be as dramatic as the "too late" in war, but it is as real to its victims, and as irrevocable; and it is bitter to reflect that it is a socialist Government which must make, indeed has already made, the tacit confession "We could have saved lives: we did not do so." The far greater guilt of the Americans is their concern, not ours.

It need not be pointed out, either, that there is something very curious about the food-stocks position. We were supposed to be down to rock bottom—see the Government "hand-out," as it is called, reprinted on page 121: but when the pressure became great enough, and when we wanted a *quid pro quo* from America, we first agreed to the diversion of 200,000 tons of wheat with a guarantee of replacement, and then forewent our "claim" on another 200,000 without a guarantee—and the position was apparently so little critical that, several weeks after the first 200,000 had gone, even bread rationing had not yet been introduced. And what of the other foods that go to make up that great total of 4 million tons? Isn't the real truth that we have stored up treasure for ourselves in order to safeguard our future standards of living, when to keep a little less would have saved people, never mind how many or how few, from dying *now*? Indeed, Mr. Attlee has admitted as much in the House of Commons.

* * * *

As to the "popular" Press, it has been, during the whole of this period, of an unscrupulous vulgarity impossible to exaggerate.

With some exceptions, it has concealed facts, told lies, magnified trivialities, and deliberately appealed to the greed, self-interest and xenophobia which are latent in almost every one of us. "Victor's Feast!" cried *The Daily Express* when our extra Christmas rations were announced: "Second Helping!" was the *Daily Mirror* headline. That was how they called us to Christ's birthday while Sir George Franckenstein was witnessing unutterable misery in Vienna, and noting in particular that fats were "sorely needed": fats the 7,000 "extra Christmas" tons of which (to say nothing of the sugar or meat) would have sufficed to provide a quarter of an ounce daily for six months to over five million of Europe's school-children. On the morning after Boxing Day *The Daily Mirror*, which I understand is read by a quarter of the population, printed what is called a "splash" article with the headline 'How can I lift my hangover?' "I expect you have all done yourselves pretty well over the holidays" it began. "Not up to pre-war standard, but well enough to be suffering some of the consequences, though maybe you don't like admitting it. . . . But to return to the common results of the Christmas festivities—diarrhœa and vomiting. What is the right thing to do?"

At the turn of the year, when the European situation was steadily worsening, a regular campaign was under weigh in several newspapers, with combined circulations running into tens of millions, for an immediate and permanent increase of rations. They had been encouraged, perhaps, by Sir Ben Smith's statement, a few days before, that "domestic rations would be increased for everyone as soon as the supply position permitted." 'Have Our Rations Gone On Too Long?' asked *The Sunday Express* at the head of a couple of columns. Next week the same journal supplied the answer: 'Not Enough Food to Keep People Fit' was the title of one main article; 'Bumper Cargoes of Food Coming: Australia beats her record' was the title of another. 'What is Wrong with our Rations?—A Warning' asked James Harpole ("The Famous Surgeon") across four columns of *The Sunday Graphic*. A leading article in *The Evening Standard* was headed, perhaps a little blasphemously, "Feed my lambs": the children referred to being exclusively British. But the climax was reached in an article "featured" by *The Daily Mail*. 'We're Starving: Let's Face It' was the headline, in letters which I have measured and find to be half an inch high and an eighth of an inch thick. The opening sentence was this: "The most profound truth ever uttered about diet occurred in a song immortalised by Marie Lloyd—'A little of what you fancy does you good'". The conclusion: "To keep this country healthy our rations should *at the very least* [emphasis in the original] be doubled. That means meat, bacon, cheese and milk, butter and margarine. It would be better for the whole country if they could triple them. If only the meat ration were to be increased, leaving all others static, it should be increased four times."

Then came the cut in dried egg and of an ounce a week in fats. There were a number of additions to balance the cuts, such as more shell-eggs and an earlier increase in the milk allowance, combined with incoming fruits and flour of a higher extraction rate: the result in fact was, as these papers perfectly well knew, to leave our calories undiminished. They also knew that the position in Europe was now desperate. But in the opinion of *The Evening Standard* "the British people feel that they have touched rock-bottom of austerity. They will tolerate no more cuts. They have gone so far, but the further must be in the direction of increases, not decreases . . . The people and the children are short of sustenance . . . the mere maintenance of the present rations is insufficient." Four days later "The people of Britain" said the same paper "see with dismay the very basis of their existence in some peril." 'Britain Getting Near the Hunger Line' was the caption in *The Sunday Graphic*. On February 8th *The Daily Express* devoted a large part of its front page to this topic. With a "banner," as I believe it is called, across seven of its eight columns it warned the public that more bad news might be coming. "No decorations on cakes and pastries" was, it seemed, one of the cuts to be feared. Minor headlines were "Women protest: we won't go on", and "'Dried eggs' shout in cinema." *The Evening News* published just under a yard of letters "Food: A Family Chorus" in a single issue; and a cartoon in *The Daily Mail* depicted Sir Ben Smith in the pillory with an empty basket round his neck, and a howling mob of *sans-culottes* flinging rolling pins at him. A knife inscribed with the word 'Bread' had missed his head by a small margin.

So I could continue. All in all, I doubt whether there has been a more dishonourable campaign in the whole history of British journalism.

2

I say, then, that the Government's first proposition—"We have all along been making every possible sacrifice"—is demonstrably false: false on the evidence of its own statistics, false in the light of its own belated actions. This being so, its second proposition—that in the general share-out our first duty is to fight for our Empire and Allies—at once becomes largely humbug. I don't mean by this that we haven't genuinely fought the Americans to secure better treatment for India than for Japan; and as to the liberated territories of Europe, we certainly did all we could to get their needs satisfied before Germany's, until a growing fear that our own administration might collapse if German rations fell below a thousand calories induced us to shift our emphasis. I mean rather that only if we ourselves had done and were doing everything possible for India and the liberated territories, only if we had really scraped the bottom of our own barrel, could we with any honesty even attempt to justify the actual starvation of Germany by reference to Allied and Imperial distress. As we have plainly done nothing of the kind, we must read the proposition with a proviso which immediately robs it of all the moral validity that in the eyes of many reasonable people it might otherwise possess. For what in the light of the facts it really means is this: "In the general share-out, we must fight for the interests of India and the liberated territories, provided that our own interests, our own relatively high standards of comfort, do not suffer." A White Paper on the World Food Shortage (Cmd. 6785) was issued at the beginning of April. It includes a table "Comparison of Current Consumption Levels (Calories per head per day)," in which the figures are grouped in a way very convenient for my purpose. The United Kingdom figure is, as we know already, 2,850; this is for the whole population, but a note is added to explain that the average for the non-farm population, which is not separately estimated, is unlikely to be significantly different. The figure for the non-farm populations of "France, Belgium, Holland, Norway" is given as 1,800/2,300: of "Unrra countries" (namely Greece, Yugoslavia, Czechoslovakia and Italy) as 1,400/1,800: and of "Ex-enemy countries" as 1,200/1,400. The ration for Germany we also know already: 1,000 for normal consumers in the British zone, who, we are told in the White Paper, "make up about half the population." The position in the Unrra countries (though not in Great Britain) has very gravely deteriorated since then, as we are aware from the statements of Mr. Hoover and Mr. LaGuardia, but even as they stand these figures are conclusive. How, or how with sincerity, could we ground our case for starving Germany on solicitude for our Allies, when some of those Allies were getting 1,400 calories, which is near-starvation, but ourselves double? And the case is really worse than that. While it is true that we have fought for our Allies against our ex-enemies, it is also true that we have fought for ourselves against our Allies. We took at Christmas, for instance, a cut of no more than 10 per cent. in wheat imports for the first half of 1946—Sir Ben Smith himself said so; but Unrra, as Mr. Lehman pointed out at the Sixth Plenary Session on March 19th, had to content itself with 53 per cent. of its bread grain requirements, and less than 4 per cent. of its edible fats requirements, for the period from January to March. And Unrra feeds our Allies. Again, "Sir Ben Smith" reported *The News Chronicle* on March 12th "is meeting solid opposition in Washington from the European importing countries. They argue that the British imports of wheat should be further cut, as we took a smaller reduction at Christmas time than did most other European States. The British reply is that European countries have no right to call on us to cut wheat imports so long as they divert a substantially greater proportion of wheat and other grain to feeding livestock than we do." Among those who were "calling on us to cut our wheat imports" but "had no right to do so" were, it appeared, France and Belgium, our Allies.

The plain fact is that "The Allies and India before Germany" is an ugly piece of *suggestio falsi*: the honest way of saying it would be "Ourselves first, the Allies and India second, and Germany next to nowhere." How then can we escape the charge of succumbing to that very vice of national self-interest which for six ghastly years we had been fighting? Lord Woolton, who had himself been Minister of Food, made a significant speech in London on February 20th: "I pledged [Sir Ben Smith] my support," he said, "on condition . . . that he would not feed the people of Europe or anyone else at the expense of our already low minimum standard of rationing in this country . . . I beg the Government not to be too internationally minded on the food front. Britain comes first with the people of this country . . ." On, I think, the very same day a remark by Goering four years before was used against him at Nuremberg: "If anyone feels hungry," he had said, "it will not be the German people . . . It makes no difference to me if the peoples you administer starve . . . this everlasting concern about foreign peoples must cease now, once and for all." Well, Lord Woolton is an English gentleman and Goering a Nazi thug, and no one imagines that Lord Woolton would deliberately starve people as Goering would and did; but, that apart, aren't the two attitudes perilously similar? And wasn't Lord Woolton giving a totally unnecessary piece of advice to a Government that entirely agreed with him?

I repeat, then, that the proposition I am discussing is half humbug. The half that isn't humbug—the belief that, if it comes to starvation, Germany and not for instance Poland ought to starve (it being always understood that we ourselves must in no event suffer)—is as devoid of any ethical basis as would be, of course, its converse. For if the Government's third proposition —that Germany must come at the end of the queue—means, as it does mean, that we should "let them starve" or "leave them to their fate", and not merely that we should refuse to share comforts after bare necessities have been met, then this proposition is grossly and obviously immoral. For my own part I go further, and believe it to be right to share comforts as well, except in so far as others, by reason of what they have suffered, have a greater need of them; but I am aware that very few even of the otherwise sympathetic would agree with me, and I have no wish to labour the point. What is vital is to establish a minimum on which responsible opinion can agree.

§ 3

There are three propositions which should, in my view, be substituted for the Government's. But before setting them down I would make, for the second time, a most urgent plea to the reader. Abandon utterly the concepts "Germany" and "India." "Germany" and "India" simply do not exist. Remember instead what does exist—so many millions of individual human beings like you and me, living in Germany and India, and with precisely the same potentiality for suffering as yours and mine. Until that truth is not merely intellectually grasped but emotionally lived with, a sane solution of the world's problems is impossible. And if you cannot get out of your mind the question of "guilt," which in fact is totally irrelevant in this connection, realise at any rate that no one but a lunatic could regard German children up to thirteen years of age—those born, that is to say, after Hitler came to power—as "guilty" of anything whatsoever. I say nothing of the German victims of Hitler's camps, or old peasant women from Silesia, or any of the others in a list that you can easily fill out for yourselves.

The three propositions which, I suggest, should have guided us, and should guide us now, are the following: (1) Quite irrespective of what other countries may or may not do, we should make the very maximum contribution in our power to the relief of suffering wherever it may occur. (2) In allocating our help the criterion should be the degree of need, and nothing else whatsoever. (3) Strictly within the context of, and subject to the limitations implied by, the second proposition, we have a special obligation to Germany.

(1) *Quite irrespective of what other countries may or may not do, we should make the very maximum contribution in our power to the relief of suffering wherever it may occur.* It would be waste of words to argue about this at the present stage. It is implied in everything I have written. If the reader is not already persuaded, I cannot hope to persuade him now.

But let me make clear, beyond any possibility of misunderstanding, what I really mean. Immensely welcome though they are, the measures so far taken—the darker loaf, fewer biscuits, a little less beer, even bread rationing if it comes—will mean nothing more than additional inconvenience for us while others are dying: they will involve, if any reduction at all in our daily calorie intake (which is improbable), then relatively a quite insignificant one. I mean, then, that so long as there are famine conditions anywhere in the world there should be an appreciable reduction in our standard of living—children, adolescents and heavy workers being excepted. I am aware that there is no possibility whatever of any such thing being done; but I am considering not what will be done, but what ought to be done if we were prepared to practise the faith we profess, and if we understood that nothing but its uncompromising practice can now save our civilisation. I shall be told also that our people wouldn't "stand for it." That I do not believe. Given the right appeal, the potentialities of men and women for good are as great as, in the other event, are their potentialities for evil.

And there is one measure to which no objection about people's unwillingness can in the nature of the case apply. A number of proposals have been put forward from time to time for voluntary sacrifice by those who feel they have something to spare. They have been summarily rejected. Worst of all is the ban on the despatch of food parcels, not only to Germany and other ex-enemy countries but anywhere abroad whatsoever: one of the objections being, if you please, that our health would suffer. Such a fear is plainly nonsensical; but even if it were not, surely moral health is at least as important as physical. Whatever may be thought of our public policy, is it tolerable that the springs of private charity should be deliberately dried up? And in this case we are lagging behind others: in the United States, for instance, there is a great drive for voluntary food collections under the chairmanship of Mr. Wallace, and the Senate has recently passed a bill permitting the despatch of private parcels to ex-enemies in Germany and Japan. Morning after morning letters come in from people whose parents are dying abroad: can't we get permission for them, they ask, to send what they are longing to send out of their own rations? We have to reply, with a terrible sense of impotent despair, that we can do nothing. Must such inhumanity continue? Even at this late hour I would appeal once more to the Prime Minister, not in my own words but in the far better ones of a lady who has sent me a copy of what she has written him: 'The world,' she says, 'has reached a point at which men's bodies can only be salvaged by swiftly-brought food, and their spirits by swiftly-shown humanity. I beg you to give us, as a nation, the power to show this humanity to our starving fellows. I beg you to grant every individual the right to spend or spare what he can for the sake of other people. The response to such a right would not only help to save some of our brothers' lives all over the earth, but would help to kindle in ourselves the soul that nations need now as they have never needed it before. Politics, and secure well-being, cannot kindle that soul, on which the future depends; sacrifice can. We held through the war because we all suffered together. We may hold through the peace, if we all suffer together, for the world cannot live without hope, and signs of love are hope to the hopeless. We know that hate is catching throughout a nation—it is my unshakeable belief that love is as catching. I beg you to liberate us, and give us the chance to prove it.'

(2) *In allocating our help the criterion should be the degree of need, and nothing else whatsoever.* This proposition is based on

one article of faith, and two undeniable facts. The article of faith is the burden of this essay: namely that human personality must be scrupulously respected, and that all human beings, irrespective of such "accidents" as their degree of virtue and what they may or may not have done to us or others, are ultimately and spiritually equal. The two undeniable facts are, first, that starvation outrages personality: if you starve a man long enough you turn him, unless he is a saint, into something very like a beast, something from which his essential humanity has departed; and secondly that for all men— black or white, Jew or Gentile, Nazi or anti-Nazi, "innocent" or "guilty"—the agony of starvation is identical. Or if it is not quite identical that is because there are certain differences which cut across all distinctions of race or nationality, virtue or wickedness, colour or creed: they are differences in fineness of nerve and sensitiveness of reaction.

As, then, the two facts are indisputable, to talk of "putting Germany at the end of the queue" is simply to deny the whole western faith of respect for personality. It would be simply impossible for anyone who called himself a liberal or a Christian to talk, not of "putting Germany," but of "putting every man and woman and child in Germany", at the end of the queue; yet it is the second phrase which means something, and something dreadful, while the first means literally nothing. I do not even wish to make the point that "to put Germany at the end of the queue" is to ignore the distinction between the obviously "innocent" and the obviously or supposedly "guilty": that it may mean, for instance, to prefer a Frenchman who has actively or passively collaborated to a German who has been tortured by Hitler's Gestapo. For to distinguish, in this matter of relief from suffering, the "innocent" and the "guilty," though better than distinguishing men of one nationality from men of another, would be quite irrelevant; such a distinction would be based in the last analysis on the *lex talionis,* which is quite inconsistent with respect for personality.

We take, then, the degree of need as our criterion. What does this mean? It means something perfectly simple. If a German is starving and a Frenchman suffering from malnutrition, and we can feed only one, we feed the German. If a German child and a French child are both suffering from malnutrition but, owing to the fact that he has been starved longer, the Frenchman's case is worse than the German's, then, again if we can feed only one, we feed the Frenchman : simply because the Frenchman's case is worse, not because it was "the Germans" who starved him. There you have the criterion of need in a nutshell : there is nothing more to it than that. To assess the degree of need may be extremely difficult, but the principle is clear ; and "putting Germany at the end of the queue" is totally opposed to it.

(3) *Strictly within the context of, and subject to the limitations implied by, this second proposition, we have a special obligation to Germany.* By this I do not for a moment mean that we should, for instance, give starving Germans a preference over starving Indians, on the ground that Germans are Europeans, or white men, or nearer to us, or for any other reason you may choose. Any such preference is absolutely forbidden by our second proposition. What I do mean can perhaps be best explained if I ask the reader to imagine for a moment that Britain and the British zone of Germany were totally isolated from the rest of the world, and that therefore help to the Germans could come from Britain alone and Britain could help only the Germans. In that event we should have an obligation, if that be possible, over and above the obligation dictated by general principles and common humanity.

Our special obligation issues from a number of facts, the chief of which are the following :

(a) We imposed unconditional surrender. There was no discussion of terms, no consideration of safeguards : the Germans were required to place themselves utterly in our hands. Their Government, we said, must go, and no new one would be allowed to take its place. By our own command, by the might of bombers that would otherwise have destroyed them to the last man, they were to be, in complete helplessness, at the mercy of their victors. I am not discussing the wisdom or morality or expediency or what you will of unconditional surrender : I am stating a fact. If that does not impose a special obligation on a nation that calls itself civilised, what does?

(b) This obligation is so absolute that nothing can make it more categorical than it just is in its own right. But for the benefit of those with whom a verbal pledge weighs more than a moral imperative, I append two statements made by Mr. Churchill, one just after he had assumed power and the other when, on the eve of the final campaign, he was begging the German people for the last time to abandon their resistance unconditionally :

August 20th, 1940. "Meanwhile we can and will arrange in advance for the speedy entry of food into any part of the enslaved area . . . so that there will always be held up before the eyes of the peoples of Europe, *including—I say deliberately—the German and Austrian peoples* [my emphasis], the certainty that the shattering of the Nazi power will bring to them all immediate food, freedom and peace."

January 18th, 1945. "I am clear that nothing should induce us to abandon the principle of unconditional surrender and enter into any form of negotiation with Germany or Japan, under whatever guise such suggestions may present themselves, until the act of unconditional surrender has been formally executed. But the President of the United States of America and I, *in your name* [my emphasis], have repeatedly declared that the enforcement of unconditional surrender upon the enemy in no way relieves the victorious Powers of their obligations to humanity, or of their duties as civilised and Christian nations. I read somewhere that when the ancient Athenians on one occasion overpowered a tribe in the Peloponnesus which had wrought them great injury by base, treacherous means, and when they had the hostile army herded on a beach naked for slaughter, they forgave them and set them free, and they said:

"'This was not done because they were men, it was done because of the nature of man.'

"Similarly in this temper one may now say to one's foes, 'We demand unconditional surrender, but you well know how strict are the moral limits within which our action is confined. We are no extirpators of nations, or butchers of peoples. We make no bargain with you. We accord you nothing as a right. Abandon your resistance unconditionally. We remain bound by our customs and our nature.'"

It was magnificently said. Has the promise been fulfilled?

(c) When the Germans were at our mercy, by our own deliberate act we made it certain that those at least of them who were in our charge, I mean the Germans of the British zone, must starve unless assistance were given. Or rather not by one act, but by three. Germany was not self-supporting in food or animal feeding stuffs before the war, as I have already mentioned in another connection. Despite six years of intensive preparation by the Nazis after 1933, and their success in raising food production to a remarkable level by the use of artificial fertilisers, mechanical equipment and a vigorous agricultural policy, Germany as a whole was still importing nearly 10 per cent. of her total requirements before September 1939. Of all the geographical regions of Germany, that now known as the British zone had easily the most unfavourable balance between consumption and production. To this zone alone were imported one and a half million tons of cereals, 200,000 tons of maize and rice, 500,000 tons of potatoes and over 1,300,000 tons of oil seeds. These imports came partly from other regions of Germany and partly from abroad.

Now what have we done—we, with our Potsdam Conference, for which we cannot evade our due share of responsibility? The facts are familiar to the reader, but they must be repeated for my present purpose. First, then, we have lopped off from Germany, and handed over to Poland, some of the richest of her food-producing territories; secondly, we have divided her into four more or less watertight zones; and thirdly by the policy of mass expulsions we have so increased the population in the British zone that today there are least 2,000,000 more mouths to feed than there were in 1939. After producing famine by our own acts, just or unjust—and for my part I think them abominably unjust—and a famine over and above what would in any case have resulted from war or acts of God, can we decently refuse to alleviate it? I hope no one will reply "But look at what they did to others." I am well aware of it. I had an intimate friend, a Frenchman and a Jew. He was a serious socialist, and at the same time full of a particularly buoyant *joie de vivre*. He had a charming wife, delicate and slender, and also very good. They both disappeared to Auschwitz, and no one ever heard of them again. No, I don't need, God knows, to be told what Hitler did. But how can such considerations for a moment be relevant? Do we want, however remotely, to follow the Nazi lead?

(d) Other suffering countries have independent Governments which can bargain to some degree at least in the world markets, and some can also draw assistance from Unrra, far too meagre though it is. Germany has no Government, and Unrra is strictly forbidden to operate there, except for displaced persons.

(e) A special obligation is involved in the relation as such of a liberal or Christian conqueror to his enemy. It is a matter of spiritual *noblesse oblige*. But I will not labour the point, for people who do not understand why St. Paul said "If thine enemy hunger, feed him" will certainly not listen to a feeble re-echo from me. The degree of need, I repeat, is the final criterion: to prefer a suffering enemy to an equally suffering friend would be wickedness: but, with that proviso, an enemy's enmity is something additionally compulsive, or would be if his hunger were not already compulsive absolutely.

*   *   *   *

I will say only one word more on this subject. The position in Germany remains, as I go to press, unchanged. Normal consumers in our zone still officially get only 1,000 calories; and though some may be able to supplement this ration by a few extra calories, millions have to live or die on it, and many of these millions get in practice even a hundred or two hundred calories less—in other words, the Belsen ration of eight or nine hundred calories. A high official of Military Government, on leave in this country, has just told me that the girls in his office are daily fainting at their desks. The ration will, I believe, be maintained; indeed the Government is probably now fighting to maintain it, not from humanitarian motives—does Mr. Attlee realise, I wonder, what it means for a socialist to have to write like this?—but because otherwise our administrative task would become totally impossible. There is so far, however, no sign of any intention to increase the ration. Now there are a round 45 million civilians in this country, and there are 10 million "normal consumers" in the British zone. It therefore follows that, as Sir Arthur Salter has pointed out in a letter to *The Times,* a reduction of our 2,850 calories—or 2,750 or whatever it may be—by an average of no more than 100 a day would lift these Germans from starvation to the level of about 1,500 calories, which is still far below the essential minimum as generally recognised. Unless by this cut in our consumption, by release of stocks (not necessarily of wheat) or by any other method you may prefer we raise them to that still wretched level, then we lose for western civilisation even such parts of Germany as can still be saved: and, what is more, there will be something in our own lives from which we can never escape, and it will not be a blessing.

VII

But food is only a part, though the most important part, of the immediate problem in Germany; and though this is primarily a short essay about morals, not a manual of what are called "practical politics," that problem cannot be left in the air. A great deal of the damage already done is irreparable : but, things being as they now are, what ought our policy to be?

1. The danger that faces us must be bluntly stated. It is that rump-Germany, at present divided into zones separately administered and with conflicting policies, will achieve unity under Soviet auspices and communist control, and in the result will be "tied up" politically and economically with the Soviet Union. Three factors will have produced this development : first, Potsdam ; second, Soviet single-mindedness ; third, our own deficiencies. The first cannot at present be altered, so far as Germany as a whole is concerned : the second can never be altered : the third can, and should, be altered immediately.

A Germany reunited in this way would be a fiercely nationalist Germany. The Vansittartites never so much as suspected, what was always as plain as the nose on my face, that this must be the result of their policy : and if Lord Vansittart himself now appears to sense rather than understand the danger, he can hardly be relied upon to draw the apppropriate conclusion.

Apart altogether from the drive to nationalism inherent in the whole present German position in its setting of previous history, the communists of all countries have long since dropped their internationalist slogans (just as Russia dropped the Internationale) and become anything from patriots to chauvinists with a semi-racialist tinge. But they have not ceased to be internationalists of a sort. There is, indeed, an intellectually amusing if morally disastrous contrast between the social democracy, such as it is, of Britain on the one hand, and the communism of Soviet Russia and elsewhere on the other. Our social democracy is, as I said at the beginning, really national socialist : though of course there are exceptions, it is almost wholly devoid of internationalist sentiment. But it is nationalist from narrow motives of self-interest, and not from any expansionist tendencies. No one could call it even remotely chauvinist. Modern communism, on the other hand, is often fiercely chauvinist ; but it is chauvinist for an international purpose, namely the spread everywhere of communism and the Soviet power. The fact simply is that in the post-war situation, when there is such a growth of nationalist sentiment at once as a result of Nazi influence and as a reaction to Nazi conquest, an appeal to nationalism is the easiest way of winning approval from the populace : and what is true of almost every country is true above all of Germany. A communist Germany would be infected with many, though not all, of the nationalist poisons that we fought the war so largely to purge.

If there is a united communist rump-Germany, it is probable that France will "go communist" too. The situation in France is more critical than most people imagine. Already the glances, not only of communists but of many socialists also, are more towards Russia than towards us; and simultaneously the Right is emerging. That is why a firm understanding with France about the Ruhr and the Rhineland, to which I shall come presently, is so vital. But, critical though the situation already is, it seems hard to imagine that western socialism could survive in France if the Soviet power were effectively established on her borders. There would not necessarily, or even probably, be a communist majority: but that there would be communist control, perhaps after a preliminary phase of right-wing domination or dictatorship, seems certain. What we should then have to face would be a sort of Moscow-Berlin-Paris axis, and Britain out of the Continent altogether. That may very well be the situation in three or four years' time, unless we mend our ways.

If that does happen, there will be two results. War between the Soviet bloc and the United States of America will have become far more probable, with ourselves as a miserable *tertium quid*. That danger is so obvious that is hardly seems worth arguing about. The second result will be that this little island will be left almost entirely alone as the standard-bearer of western values. The outposts of western civilisation on the Continent of Europe will be quite ineffective: and the United States, under the impact of growing hostility with the Soviet Union, may very well develop a set of highly illiberal traits. I have purposely said very little about the United States in this essay: but it seems to me clear that, hardly touched as she is by socialist ideas, and in the blazing flush of her arrogant capitalism, she can hardly be relied upon for the preservation of those liberal values which, strong though they have been in her, must (I say it again) all but completely vanish unless they are given a socialist realisation.

2. What, in this situation, should we do? The answer seems to me inescapable, and nothing is to be gained by running away from it. With Potsdam as our iniquitous bond, we have been haggling with our Allies for months over the economic future of rump-Germany *as a whole;* and while we have been doing so

the economic and political divergencies between the zones have rapidly increased, the Russian zone—Soviet Germany—has obviously "gone", and our own zone is drifting to ruin. The process has become self-contradictory to a grotesque degree— except on the Soviet side; and if we persist with it the result can only be the total loss not only of all Germany but of France also. While not abandoning, therefore, the hope of ultimate German unity, remote though that must seem as things are developing, we should now pursue a very different policy. It should be two-fold. First, we should aim at saving as much of Germany as possible for western civilisation by creating economic prosperity and fostering democratic self-government in our own zone, whatever other people may be doing in theirs; and secondly we should urgently seek a better understanding and closer asso- ciation with France. We should make every effort to secure Soviet cooperation with both parts of this policy, but it should be pursued unconditionally.

3. To take the French issue first. I am not one of those who favour the internationalisation of the Ruhr and Rhineland for its own sake, either as a measure of security or as a step in the direction of a United States of Europe. I don't think it the best way to get security : nor do I think that if conquerors forcibly internationalise a key area of the conquered this has anything whatever to do with international socialism or European unification. Socialists who do think so are not, I fear, the men they were six years ago. Further, I am certain that, in what- ever form, internationalisation will to some degree foster German chauvinism. Nevertheless, I cannot see that without a measure of internationalisation friendship with France can now be obtained : and if we fail to obtain it democratic socialism will surely be engulfed there, by a wave from the left or the right or both. The question then is, what measure of inter- nationalisation?

" I want for the Ruhr " says Professor Cole in his recent pamph- let* " an internationally appointed Commission of Development and Control, specifically instructed to develop the production of the region to the fullest extent that can be made consistent with the absolute prohibition of armament manufacture. . . . I want the Commission to be instructed to develop the Ruhr's resources as an international asset . . . as trustee for the participating countries,

---

* *Labour's Foreign Policy*, by G. D. H. Cole. *New Statesman & Nation*, 1946.

of which Germany as a whole should from the outset be one. I want the Commission to plan the output of the Ruhr from this standpoint. . . . I want the Commission, just as far as may be necessary for these purposes and no farther, to exercise political as well as economic control. . . . I want the Ruhr workers to be free to belong to the same Trade Unions and other democratic associations as other Germans, and, if they will, to the same political parties. . . .I am not proposing that the Commission for the Ruhr should be controlled by the countries of Western Europe alone, because any such plan would necessarily arouse the most violent opposition on the part of the Soviet Union. Economically, the development of the Ruhr and its industries must be made a matter in which all Europe has a recognised interest. . . ."

The dots I have inserted represent the omission of some key-features in Professor Cole's plan: what is left is common ground among all who support internationalisation, reluctantly or otherwise. For the rest, I would fight for the following: (i) The Commission should not control consumer industries. (ii) The political control should be confined within the narrowest limits, which should be exactly defined. (iii) There should be the strongest possible German representation on the Commission. (iv) In particular, the trade union movement of the Ruhr should be represented. (v) Production controlled by the Commission should be distributed according to percentages among all European nations, including Germany. These percentages should be fixed annually, and before they are fixed every European nation should be heard. The German percentage, which should be as high as possible, should be considered as an addition to the general figure of production laid down by the Control Council. (vi) The actual management of the industries, which should of course be collectivised, should be in German hands: foreigners should only supervise and control. (vii) The Commission should be under German law, especially in matters of taxation and labour.

These provisions would do something towards preventing an upsurge of German nationalism. Better still would be a widening of the international control to include the mining and heavy industries in Lorraine and Luxemburg, and in parts of northern France, Belgium, and southern Holland: for these form, with the corresponding industries of the Rhineland, Ruhr and Saar, a natural economic unit. If this were done, we should have, instead of a mere conqueror's dictate masquerading as internationalism, a genuine piece of international planning and a step towards European unification.

The steady aim should be an increasing integration, economic and cultural, of western Europe, with at the same time a maximum of that political independence and sovereignty which nationalist sentiment at present demands, but will not demand, we hope, for ever. This is, if you like, the policy of the western *bloc*, comprising at least Britain, France, Belgium, Holland and western and southern Germany : a *bloc*, however, neither exclusive in sentiment nor even remotely autarchic in economy. The communists of all countries denounce it fiercely : it is directed against the Soviet Union, they insist, and will mean war. Not to reply with an easy *tu quoque* I say, first, that it is not directed against the Soviet Union, for no one but a lunatic wants another war, and the number of lunatics, at any rate certified, is comparatively small : and secondly that it is far less likely to mean war than would the Moscow-Berlin-Paris axis to which I have referred.

4. Meanwhile we should immediately reverse our policy throughout the whole of the British zone, and aim, as I have said, at creating economic prosperity and fostering democratic self-government. I will say nothing further about food. For the rest, our policy has been characterised by four main features, though there have been so many contradictions that no really clear picture can be painted. But in general, first, we have combined a great deal of energy, devotion, technical skill, fair mindedness and patient administration of the colonial type—especially in the early days, when the British Army did a really magnificent job of practical relief and rehabilitation—with much arbitrariness, superiority, and failure (a far less serious failure, of course, than in the Russian zone) to respect civil liberties. Secondly, there has been hopeless confusion between Montgomery and Norfolk House, between the civil and military administration, which has been the fault of neither but must be attributed to the lack of any clear-cut Cabinet direction. Thirdly, our approach to the problems of party politics, trade unionism and self-government has been, over the period as a whole, quite unsatisfactory. Fourthly, we have had neither strategy nor tactics for such a measure of economic recovery as even within the limits of the *Potsdamer Diktat* might be possible. To take these points in order :

(a) Colonialism must go.   What I mean by colonialism can be understood from this article by *The Manchester Guardian's* Berlin correspondent, dated May 1st 1946:

"There is a peculiar British approach towards conquest which holds subtle and very real dangers for those carrying out the British share of the occupation of Germany.   This can perhaps best be described as 'the habit of mind of the British Raj.'

"It is an old problem with us, and we have seen its evil effects over and over again in India.   The 'Raj mentality,' self-satisfied, selfish, sanctimonious, spread across the generations of our connection with India, has done, perhaps, more than anything else to create Indian irritation and to offset the immense value of the good that we have achieved in India.   There are ominous signs of the Raj appearing now in Germany.   We may be able to correct many mistakes of occupation policy in Germany as time goes on, but there is one mistake that we shall never be able to overcome if we once begin to make it seriously: this is, to treat the Germans as a colonial people.

"The core and very heart of the Raj is 'the club,' and 'the club,' with all its familiar trappings and familiar brittle conversation, is appearing wherever the British have begun to settle down in Germany.   N.A.A.F.I. is austere enough with tobacco that costs dollars and with little luxuries that have to come from England, but there is nothing austere in British requisitioning of lavish German palaces for clubs, nor of stocks of German gin and any wines available.   At the Atlantic Hotel in Hamburg, at the Embassy Club in Berlin, and even at the numerous smaller clubs that exist wherever there are enough British forces gathered to maintain them, Service officers, both men and women, and Control Commission civilians of 'officer status' can enjoy a style of living that in England exists only for the very rich and in India or the colonies has been regarded as the natural perquisite of 'the sahib.'   The Raj is specifically a danger of those of 'officer status'; indeed, the fine distinctions of 'status' are essential to maintain it.

"Now, there is nothing wrong in the provision of attractive clubs for men and women doing the work and leading the often dreary life of occupation in Germany, and it is far from the intention of this article to criticise the existence of British officers' clubs as such.   But one cannot help being struck not only by the immeasurable difference between the luxury of many of these clubs and the standards of living of the surrounding German people but also—and the contrast is important—by the difference between these clubs and almost anything that can normally be enjoyed in England. There are two dangers here: first, the power of the club to create an illusion that the Germans are an inferior and backward people, and, secondly, the dangerous contrast between life in England, where luxury has to be worked for, if it can be obtained at all, and Germany, where, for the British, it can be requisitioned.

" Just as a foreign 'white man' could always count on the hospitality of a British club in India, so an Allied national can be entertained in British clubs in Germany. But no German may enter one of these clubs other than as a servant. The Americans have some restaurants or messes to which Germans may be invited; the British have so far set their face against this sternly."

This almost caste superiority, if persisted in, must evoke in those subjected to it just the complex of qualities that we are presumably most anxious not to evoke—self-contempt, hatred, aggressiveness and servility. It should be replaced by the contrary attitude: by the sense that we are in Germany to cooperate with the Germans, at least on terms of equal respect, in trying to save as much as we can from the ruin of their country. Habeas corpus must be as much of a reality as it is in England. At least those Germans who have proved themselves active anti-Nazis—Military Government has their names—should be freed from humiliating restrictions: they should not be subject to the curfew and ban on foreign newspapers, they should be allowed to move where they please, their contacts with Military Government personnel should be quite unfettered, and in general they should have just the same privileges as those granted to British or Allied civilians. In view of the appalling housing situation, to say nothing of the famine, such wretched inhumanities as the contemplated seizure of German dwelling-places to accommodate the wives of the British military should no longer be considered.

(b) At the start, when the war had only just come to an end and affairs were much confused, a strictly military government was no doubt the only possible way of ensuring the maintenance of any kind of order. This was all very well, but military government in fact continued far too long, and, with lack of any kind of real direction from the Cabinet, local military commanders were allowed far too much personal power to do more or less what they pleased in the towns or districts they governed. The result was that in one area trade unions might be encouraged and local trade union leaders given a good deal of scope to organise their activities, while across some arbitrary border in a neighbouring district trade unionism was given no scope at all. On April 15th this strictly military set-up was changed, and from that date the Control Commission in its civil aspect under Mr. John Hynd assumed direct responsibility for the government of the British zone. This meant that local area commanders, while still for the most part military men, came directly under the Control Office, and the Corps Commanders, who had been in the position of almost absolute governors for their Corps areas, reverted to a purely military status and with control only over the occupation tasks of our military forces. Since then a group of civilian Regional Commissioners has been appointed to take over what amounts to the governorship of the various provinces in the British zone. This in theory will strengthen the civilian handling of military government affairs in Germany, but in practice, since most of the staffs of these Regional Commissioners and their seconds-in-command will probably remain military, far too much must depend on the individual personality of the Regional Commissioner. What is needed is a much more direct interest by the Cabinet in our affairs in Germany, and a much more effective liaison between the Control Office in London and the men who interpret its decisions on the spot.

(c) Our approach to the whole question of party politics has been timid in the extreme. While the Russians have supported the communists in their zone, and indeed in all the others, to the top of their bent, we have been frightened, consciously or unconsciously, of giving more than the most tepid encouragement to the social democrats in ours. But they are the strongest party in our zone, or certainly were until the recent ration "cut": they alone can establish a western-socialist régime: the alternative is either communism of the Soviet type or neofascism: so why on earth, it must be asked, have we been hesitating? I am not, of course, suggesting any undemocratic procedure, or methods even remotely resembling those that the Soviet Union is employing to secure predominance for the communists: what I am suggesting is that British labour should give really warm-hearted and fraternal encouragement to its brother party in Germany, and that this encouragement should not be neutralised by the attitude or actions of men on the spot. What is wanted is nothing more than a wholly legitimate cooperation. But that this cooperation may be fruitful, our political and economic policy must be such that self-respecting Germans can honestly cooperate in it : otherwise they run the risk of becoming quislings, and of being despised as such. Nor must we " use " the social democrats as mere instruments of our own nationalist policies. There are indications that at the moment our attitude to them is becoming much more positive ; and it is difficult not to connect this change with the Russian campaign for " working-class unity." But while the change itself is to be most warmly welcomed, we must beware of playing the social demo-crats as pawns in the game of " power politics ". To strengthen western values for their own sake is one thing : to use exponents of them as means to our private ends is not merely another thing, but the opposite. In the first case we are meeting the rivalry of communism, as we should and must meet it, by removing hin-drances to the liberal way of life : in the second, we are simply opposing British to Soviet nationalism.

Most important of all, we should foster trade unionism of the really effective type, with full bargaining powers, and should hand over to Germans a rapidly increasing measure of self-government. Is democratic self-government our aim in Germany, or isn't it? If it isn't, we are simply perpetuating the paternalism, the lack of civic initiative, which, we are always saying, has brought the Germans to their present pass. If it is, why don't we get on with it? The re-education effected by responsibility is worth all other sorts of re-education, bogus or genuine, put together. Moreover, if we deny these men responsibility they will look more and more to the East, where German communists will be increasingly in control. Indeed, in spite of everything they dislike in the Soviet administration they are already doing so.

I shall be told that effective self-government has already begun. No. The Nominated Councils set up by us at the local govern-ment level are petty affairs of very limited democratic value ; and as to the Zonal Advisory Council, officially described as " a start on the higher levels of government ", this is what " Peregrine ", the famous *Observer* correspondent, wrote to his paper from Hamburg on April 13th 1946 :

" Even now the Zonal Advisory Council—the nucleus of a German administration for the British zone—has far less power than any local council in any remote parish in any other coun-try. Even its internal discussions, conducted behind closed doors, are strictly controlled by Military Government to such an extent that the Council's members, while in conference, are forbidden to discuss some of the most vital issues concerning the economic life of the British zone. The result of this is a growing despondency even among those anti-Nazi leaders who had set all their hopes on cooperation with British democracy. They now feel more and more like helpless puppets of a foreign Power surrounded by the hostility of their own people."

A remark made recently by an anti-Nazi German of strong British sympathies accurately sums up the position. "Why don't you practise democracy" he asked "instead of talking so much about it?" Not that we have talked about it effectively. Without resorting to the kind of propaganda which always and quite properly antagonises people, we could have done a great deal to familiarise the Germans with western conceptions of democracy by sending in British newspapers, publishing British books in translation, and producing British plays. We have done nothing of the kind. Germans are not allowed to buy our newspapers, and offers of free copies to German journalists, universities and schools are refused. About books it is difficult to speak without impatience. Haven't we the imagination to realise how drab and dull and hopeless are these Germans' lives, and how eager so many of them must be to escape into the absorptions of literature? Why don't we make it easy for them to do so? No one seems to know what our policy is: but whatever it may be the shortage of books amounts to a famine. I had repeated requests for a German edition of Gedye's "Fallen Bastions"—a book as passionately anti-Nazi as any written in any language since Hitler first started his campaign. I made application: it was refused. The book, I suspect, was "too political."

As to German newspapers produced under Allied control, those of the British zone are the dullest and most uninspiring in the whole country. They are not, it is true, mere propaganda sheets like those produced by the Russians; but they lack the liveliness and the atmosphere of criticism and free discussion that characterises the newspapers for which the Americans are responsible. It is not surprising that the American-published *Neue Zeitung* has, in consequence, become Germany's most important newspaper, with a circulation of between two and three million. Moreover, while Russia has made available great quantities of paper for the expression of communist opinion, the Liberals and Social

Democrats of our zone have had the greatest difficulty in securing adequate supplies of newsprint for the expression of theirs. Such niggardliness is culturally suicidal.

(d) The Russians have had a perfectly clear strategy of land reform (needlessly cruel though in many ways it has been) and industrial socialisation. Our failure in such matters has been complete. "This negative approach in economic reconstruction" says *The Economist* of April 6th 1946, and the position could not be put more clearly "is illustrated by the fact that the only important change in the structure of German industry in the British zone—the expropriation of the coal owners—has not been followed by the elaboration of a positive alternative. In the steel industry the change has again been limited to the negative action of imprisoning the leading industrialists. Otherwise, the business world is left, virtually without direction or purpose, to reopen its stock exchanges and chambers of commerce, and to manipulate as best it may an economy half in ruins and half earmarked for reparations." This is indeed an understatement. The chambers of commerce are positively favoured relatively to the trade unions. Many of them have been allowed to publish regional papers, whereas there is only one trade union paper in the whole zone.

Is it possible to conceive an insanity more extreme than this literally hopeless policy of economic drift? Is it any wonder that, as I am told by German social-democratic leaders whose good faith cannot be questioned, even Germans in our zone most opposed to Soviet ideas are beginning to look to the East, and to say "There, economically at least, there seems some hope"? For they know that the factory chimneys are smoking there, and that the Russians are sending in raw material and leaving a small part of the product in Germany.

The nationalisation of key industries and all-over economic planning—that is what is wanted in the British zone, and wanted as a matter of extreme urgency. In a word, a genuinely socialist policy wholeheartedly applied. A year after the end of hostilities there is still no basis on which western Germany can build, still no future for which a German with any sense of responsibility can work or hope. Instead, a total uncertainty paralyses all economic and political life.

Apart from the question of nationalisation, something very mysterious is going on in the British zone of which I have been quite unable to discover the explanation. Not to overstate, we do not appear to be fostering reconstruction even within the limits which, on a reasonable interpretation of Potsdam and even before the final decisions of March 28th, might have been considered permissible. There are rumours of industrial enterprises suddenly closed down, and the workers sacked, with no reason given : and there are rumours, also, of a small horde of British industrialists watching things, and maybe doing things, on the spot. Such rumours would in any case be inevitable, and I hope they are false : but I am bound to say that some of my information is pretty factual. Perhaps a list could be published of British economic controllers at zonal and regional headquarters and in the field, together with their industrial background, if any : unreasonable doubts might then be set at rest. It is natural, of course, that these gentlemen should travel around in the uniform of Military Government officers, for part of their job is to "spot" tit-bits for reparation. But it would not be so proper if they had any personal interest in the affair ; and while open negotiations on the basis of a clear-cut policy are one thing, any bargaining in the present twilight of "unconditional" powers, with no right of appeal, would be quite another.

If I thought that there might be even a case or two of German industry—light industry as well as heavy industry—being thwarted for fear of its potential competition with British industry, and if I further believed that the Government was turning a blind eye to such procedure, I should be confirmed in my view that this is predominantly a national socialist and not a socialist administration. That America should see Germany as a happy hunting-ground is no doubt natural, and when we read of attempts to keep the German automobile industry down because America makes cars, or German rayon and staple fibre down because America sells cotton, we are not astonished ; but for British socialism to do likewise would be to reduce our domestic revolution of summer 1945 to a mere matter of ins and outs.

*   *   *   *

The most important point remains. Mr. Churchill should never have consented, willingly or unwillingly, to the Potsdam decisions ; Mr. Attlee should never have signed them ; the agreement of March 28th should never have been made. Unless this agreement can be revised at a reasonably early date, and before the damage it must cause has become quite irreparable, we should give notice that we do not intend to apply it, or that we intend to apply it with radical modifications, in the British zone. There would be nothing in the least dishonourable about this, for the agreement is based on three fundamental assumptions, and when accepting the plan the British representative on the co-ordinating committee made a formal statement regarding these assumptions. This statement, it was added, in no way represented a reservation against the plan "provided the principle of review was recognised." Two of the assumptions were that Germany would be treated as an economic unit, and that the population would not exceed 66,500,000. Everyone knows that this figure is an underestimate by millions: and as to economic unity, there is no sign of it being even on the border-line of realisation. Unless it is realised quickly, we should have the strongest case for refusing to operate the agreement of March 28th, and for going straight ahead to apply in our zone the principles of liberal socialism which it is our duty to safeguard, and which can alone save Europe from sliding down into increasing misery, endemic lawlessness, and so, eventually, a war far more fearful and demoralising even than the last.

VIII

I have criticised in this essay our treatment of Germany. It cannot be criticised too strongly : for these policies for which we have been jointly or solely responsible—annexations, expulsions, spoliation, economic enslavement, non-fraternisation and starvation—are more in the spirit of the Hitler we fought than in that of the western liberalism for which we fought him. But to go on to suggest that all distinction has vanished, and that we have been utterly corrupted by the thing we have been fighting—this would be to exaggerate, and grossly. We have alienated great territories of the enemy : Hitler would have annexed all Europe, and eventually the whole world. We non-fraternised with the Germans : Hitler murdered six million Jews. We are starving the people in our charge, not deliberately but because to feed them as we ought would be to lower our own standards : Hitler would have starved, and did starve, anyone it might suit him to starve, with complete deliberation and even,

God forgive him, as a matter of preference. These are vast differences, and we must cling to the thought of them if we are to retain our self-respect. But it is a measure of the peril in which we stand that we can take comfort only from reflections such as these.

I have criticised many other things in our national life, and I have criticised the Labour Government. I am a more passionate socialist than ever I was, as I hope to have shown: but the essential battle today is not between capitalism and mere socialism as such, but between the liberal or Christian ethic, of which humanistic socialism is the crown, and totalitarianism in all its forms. I owe a loyalty to that ethic far greater than my loyalty to any Government that may come and go—even to a Government which, in spite of everything that can be charged against it, has already some noble achievements to its credit.

But it is not on a note of criticism that I would wish to end. Love of country is a curious thing; as in other sorts of love, it attributes qualities to the beloved which may not in fact be there. But I cannot escape the conviction, when all has been said, that there are in this country reserves of moral leadership that can still save the world, if only we can rise to the full height of the argument.

There are things that it does not become a man to say in his own person, but that he may report in the words of another. My friends from the Continent, and not from Germany or other defeated countries alone, have often told me that when they land on an English shore or at an English airport they feel they have come to Paradise. They are not referring to our food, or our law and order, or our relative prosperity: they are thinking of our freedom, of our—may I say it?—decency, of, in Mr. Churchill's words, "our customs and our nature". In spite of everything I have written, I do believe that they are right: I do believe that, corrupted though we may be by war and its aftermath, there is still something in the air we breathe, still some moral source deep in our cities and our countryside, which no other people in the modern world has the good fortune to possess. Am I falling, then, at the end into the chauvinism, if only a spiritual one, that I have condemned so often? I do not think so: but if so I cannot help it.

We face a moral crisis graver, perhaps, than the physical crisis of the war. There are two paths for the human race, and it must choose between them. One, that of greed and hatred and self-interest, will end by turning us, with or without the atom bomb, into something less than human : the other may take us, or our children's children, to heights of splendour— in body and mind and spirit—of which today we can hardly dream. Cannot we lead men, and quickly, to the better of these paths? It would not be an unEnglish thing to do. It was an English poet who wrote

> "Oh, cease! must hate and death return?
>   Cease! must men kill and die?
> Cease! drain not to its dregs the urn
>   Of bitter prophecy.
> The world is weary of the past,
> Oh, might it die or rest at last!"